Essential Histories

The Jacobite Rebellion
1745–46

Essential Histories

The Jacobite Rebellion
1745–46

Gregory Fremont-Barnes

First published in Great Britain in 2011 by Osprey Publishing
PO Box 883, Oxford, OX1 9PL, UK
1385 Broadway, 5th Floor, New York, NY 10018, USA
Email: info@ospreypublishing.com

A CIP catalogue record for this book is available from the
British Library

Print ISBN: 978 1 84603 992 8

Gregory Fremont-Barnes has asserted his right under the
Copyright, Designs and Patents Act, 1988, to be identified as the
Author of this Work.

Page layout by The Black Spot
Index by Alan Thatcher
Typeset in Gill Sans and ITC Stone Serif
Maps by Peter Bull Art Studio and the Map Studio
Originated by PPS Grasmere, Leeds, UK
Printed and bound in India by Replika Press Private Ltd.

19 20 21 22 23 10 9 8 7 6 5 4

Osprey Publishing is supporting the Woodland Trust, the UK's
leading woodland conservation charity, by funding the dedication
of trees.

www.ospreypublishing.com

Contents

Introduction   7

Chronology   10

Background to war
The roots of Jacobitism   12

Warring sides
The armies of two kings   24

Outbreak
The Bonnie Prince's rebellion   31

The fighting
Raising the standard of revolt   36

Portrait of a soldier
Lord George Murray   63

How the war ended
The battle of Culloden   67

Portrait of a civilian
Flora MacDonald   75

The world around war
Highland life in the mid-18th century   79

Conclusion and consequences   85

Further Reading   92

Index   94

Introduction

The Jacobite Rebellion of 1745 represents both a tragic episode in Scottish history and the greatest crisis to threaten British internal security in the 18th century. At once bold and brilliant, and marked by the leadership of the young, adventurous 'Bonnie Prince Charlie', the rebellion sought to restore the Stuart dynasty to the British throne, and it placed its principal hopes for success on those somewhat improbably romantic icons, the Highland clans, whose very way of life changed forever with the disaster at Culloden, the culminating battle of the rebellion.

Seen as a whole, the events of 1745–46 reveal a period of brief Jacobite triumph followed by a slow and inevitable decline, of a cause struggling against the tide of history. When James II died in 1701, those committed to the restoration of the Stuarts naturally transferred their loyalties to his son, James Edward Stuart and, later, to his son, Charles Edward. But unless Charles' adherents could persuade their fellow countrymen – not merely in Scotland but across Britain generally – that their claimant had no intention to re-establish the arbitrary powers once exercised by his grandfather, James II – powers stripped from him as a result of the 'Glorious Revolution' of 1688–89 – the prospect of a Stuart Restoration remained remote, if not impossible.

The Jacobite struggle is aptly named – as a rebellion, not a revolution or a civil war – for the movement sought to change the sovereign of a state, not to overturn its political system altogether, and it did not involve the great mass of the population in the manner so characteristic of revolutionary movements. While it centred on Scotland, it sought, though in fact drew relatively little, support from across the British Isles, and thus never deteriorated into a large-scale civil or internecine conflict. Its span as a political movement, influenced by religious prejudices and manifesting itself in arms three times

in the course of 60 years, traced its origins to the Glorious Revolution of 1688 when the Protestant King William III of the Netherlands deposed James II of England and effectively ended in 1746 with the collapse of the Jacobite cause at Culloden – notwithstanding the spate of insignificant conspiracies and cabals which followed over the succeeding generation.

The name 'Jacobite' derives from the Latin *Jacobus*, for James, referring to those who supported the cause of James II.

William, Duke of Cumberland. The random element of violence in the immediate aftermath of Culloden contributed less to the victors' reputation for ruthlessness than the systematic campaign of terror which followed over succeeding months. The Jacobites, as rebels, did not enjoy the privileges accorded to soldiers of conventional armies – a distinction which government troops used as mitigation for numerous acts of barbarity. (Author's collection)

Only in this respect does it satisfy a single definition, for it very rapidly assumed various associations, not least with Roman Catholicism and specifically the Highland Scots' adherence to the House of Stuart. Having said this, Jacobites were never exclusively Catholic – Protestant and Catholic Jacobites served the cause in both the risings of 1715 and 1745; nor was the movement confined to Scotland or peculiar to the Highlands. True, this rather amorphous concept has become most closely associated with the Scottish Highlands, for this was the key source of its military support, but the phenomenon also existed to a great extent on the Continent, particularly amongst émigré Scots and Irish, as well as in Ireland and in parts of England, particularly in the North, the West Country and in London.

The appeal of the '45 is more than obvious. This conflict of David and Goliath proportions, fought over a virtually hopeless cause, has manifested itself in an almost mournful admiration of the underdog – the Highland clans, dressed in their characteristic garb and armed with weapons peculiar to their region, flocking to the banner of their exiled prince. All struggles between a people conceived as semi-civilized and those of a more advanced society carry with them an element of pathos, not least when they hail from forbidding, isolated lands whose barren mountains, rugged sea coasts and remote islands forbade extensive exploration, much less development. The Highlanders, living apart from what even their Lowland cousins regarded as civilization, distinguished themselves not merely by geography but by distinctive dress, language and tribal custom, and they pursued an existence seemingly beyond the reach of established religion, to say nothing of external political authority. To many they seemed the barbaric remains of Scotland's medieval past, their way of life punctuated by military prowess, a hostile temperament and generational feuds; in short, an aberration in an era of progressive thought, technology and science inaugurated by the Enlightenment.

General Wade, later to command a government army in the campaigns of

1745–46, first encountered this society in 1724, when King George I sent him north to study the Highlanders' life, customs and economy. What he discovered only reinforced prevailing attitudes across Britain: that the Highlanders were a backward, almost savage people – paternalistic, bellicose and tribal. 'Their Notions of Virtue and Vice are very different from the more civilized part of Mankind,' he reported.

They think it a most Sublime Virtue to pay a Servile and Abject Obedience to the Commands of their Chieftains, altho' in opposition to their Sovereign, and the laws of the Kingdom…

The Virtue next to this, in esteem amongst them, is the Love they bear to that particular Branch of which they are a part, and in a Second Degree to the whole Clan, or Name, by assisting each other (right or wrong) against any other Clan

with whom they are at Variance, and great Barbarities are often committed by One, to revenge the Quarrels of Another. They have still a more extensive adherence one to another as Highlanders in opposition to the People who Inhabit the Low Countries, whom they hold in the utmost Contempt, imagining them inferior to themselves in Courage, Resolution and the use of Arms…

On the other hand, the Highland clansmen were not a race of noble savages, taken advantage of by the ambitions of the Stuarts and trampled underfoot by the forces of progress and modernity. For many chiefs, the slow movement for change threatened the clan system, and by adhering to the Stuart cause they sought to prolong their power base and the cultural system on which it rested. In truth, if the Stuarts found them a useful ally in pursuing their ends, equally the Highlanders used the Prince as a means of preserving a way of life perceived to be under threat.

Thus, study of the Jacobite Rebellion would scarcely command the interest that it enjoys stripped of its fascinating association with this remarkable people – unquestionably more feared than admired by their contemporaries and trapped in a bygone era – who violently eschewed the social and political changes well underway to the south.

The Jacobites at Prestonpans. While this marked the high point of their campaign, rebel success required more than one or two tactical victories. Much of the failure of the '45 may be attributed to the fact that Charles could only depend on a minority of Scots to support his cause. Even within the Highlands, many clans remained loyal to the government or in any event did not lend active support to the Jacobites. (Mary Evans Picture Library)

Chronology

1745 **5 July** Prince Charles Edward Stuart leaves Belle Isle, off the French coast, and sails for Scotland

9 July Naval encounter between the French warship *L'Elisabeth* (64) and HMS *Lion* (64)

25 July Prince lands on the west coast at Loch nan Uamh in Arisaig, near Moidart

6 August Prince writes to Louis XV requesting assistance

19 August Standard of revolt raised at Glenfinnan on Loch Shiel; various clans begin to assemble

21–29 August Prince proceeds east, moving between Forts William and Augustus; General Cope, commander of government forces in Scotland, marches north from Stirling for Fort Augustus before changing direction and marching to Inverness

27 August Rendezvous at Aberchalder

29 August Jacobites fail to take Ruthven Barracks

30 August–4 September Charles marches to Blair Castle and Perth, where he receives reinforcements and appoints Lord George Murray and the Duke of Perth joint commanders of his forces; Cope, aware of the Prince's movements, marches from Inverness to Aberdeen to ship his troops to Edinburgh

17 September Cope disembarks troops at Dunbar, east of Edinburgh; Jacobites occupy Edinburgh, but the castle remains in possession of the government

21 September Jacobite victory in the battle of Prestonpans

25 September Jacobites occupy Aberdeen

October Charles's army exceeds 5,000

men through continued recruitment, with Lord George Murray responsible for training and organization; Duke of Cumberland and some of his forces recalled from Flanders for service against the Jacobites; in England, Field Marshal Wade assembles troops at Newcastle; new regiments raised and militia called out; loyal Highland clans form new regiments

7 October French vessel runs the blockade and lands arms at Montrose; further ships arrive by the end of the month, supplying six pieces of artillery and other weapons

31 October Jacobite army proceeds south from Edinburgh with a view to sparking a sympathetic uprising in England and encouraging a French landing in support

10–15 November Siege of Carlisle; garrison of militia capitulates on 15th

20 November Jacobite forces march south from Carlisle towards Manchester via Preston but fail to recruit substantial numbers of adherents

24 November French troops land at Montrose

25 November HMS *Hazard* surrenders to the French and Jacobites at Montrose

26 November Lord John Drummond and Scottish troops in French service disembark at Montrose; Irish troops land at Peterhead and Aberdeen

29 November Jacobites occupy Manchester

1–4 December Main Jacobite army moves west while Murray conducts a feint to the west to distract Duke of Cumberland, then in Staffordshire; Murray succeeds in attracting Cumberland towards Stafford, then

rejoins Charles in Derby
4 December Jacobites enter Derby
6 December With no evidence of
a revolt by English Jacobites or a
French invasion, Charles orders
a retreat to Scotland
8–16 December Retreat proceeds
towards Penrith via Wigan and Kendal;
Duke of Cumberland pursues and
Wade seeks to intercept, but fails to
catch Jacobites at Wigan; further north,
Lord Loudoun occupies Inverness
18 December Engagement at Clifton
20 December Jacobite army crosses the
border into Scotland, leaving a garrison
in Carlisle Castle
21–30 December Jacobites
unsuccessfully defend Carlisle
23 December Government troops
defeated at Inverurie
25 December Jacobites reach Glasgow
30 December Carlisle surrenders to
Cumberland, who then returns to
London, leaving General Hawley
to pursue Charles's army

1746 **4 January** Charles's forces join with
those under Lord John Drummond
7–8 January Siege of Stirling; town
capitulates to the Jacobites but the
castle remains in government hands
8–31 January Jacobites continue the
siege of Stirling, ultimately failing to
take the castle; General Hawley
concentrates his force at Edinburgh,
combining with the garrison already in
situ and Wade's troops from Newcastle
14 January Hawley marches to relieve
Stirling via Linlithgow and Falkirk;
Murray moves against Hawley, leaving
a small force in vicinity of Stirling
17 January Battle of Falkirk
18–28 January Jacobites make no
inroads at the siege of Stirling and
many desert; Cumberland proceeds
north to assume command in Scotland,
entering Edinburgh on the 30th
1 February Persuaded of the futility of
the siege and aware of desertions, the
Prince retreats with his army into the

Highlands for the winter; Ruthven
Barracks surrender
4 February Cumberland pursues
Jacobite army north; Loudoun
fortifies Inverness
6 February Cumberland reaches Perth
but obliged to halt by adverse weather
16 February Lord Loudoun fails in
attempt to capture Charles in a night
raid at Moy Castle
18 February Outnumbering Loudoun's
forces, advancing Jacobites oblige him
to abandon Inverness
19–20 February Jacobite army
concentrates in and around Inverness
27 February Cumberland reaches
Aberdeen but halts to await
improved weather
3–5 March Siege of Fort Augustus;
garrison capitulates
10–31 March Jacobites unsuccessfully
besiege Blair Castle
20 March Skirmish at Dornoch;
skirmish at Keith
20 March–2 April Siege of Fort William,
which Jacobites fail to take
8 April Cumberland marches from
Aberdeen
12 April Government forces cross the
river Spey and fight the Jacobite
rearguard at Nairn on the 14th
15 April Jacobites fail to surprise
government camp at Nairn
16 April Battle of Culloden
18 April Charles's forces disperse at Fort
Augustus and Ruthven Barracks
19 April Remaining French units lay
down their arms
April (post-Culloden) to September
Cumberland suppresses all remaining
pockets of resistance in a campaign
marked by brutality and vengeance;
the government executes many
prisoners, but transports most to North
American colonies; loyal forces search
unsuccessfully for Charles across the
western Highlands and islands
27 May Last Jacobite units disband
20 September Prince departs for France
from Loch nan Uamh

The roots of Jacobitism

The origins of the Jacobite movement may be traced to the Glorious Revolution of 1688–89, when James VII of Scotland (James II of England) abdicated in favour of William of Orange as King of Great Britain. James ruled as a Catholic over a predominantly Protestant country, which – although always likely to be problematic – proved particularly unpopular while simultaneously in France, religious persecution of Protestants reached a high point. The mere fact of the king's preference for what since the Reformation had amounted to an alien faith did not fully account for the widespread suspicion he

attracted from his subjects. The Catholic king also alienated many of his subjects by extending preferential treatment to his co-religionists, and drove an otherwise religiously tolerant 17th-century society to its limits by allowing not only Catholics but also Dissenters to hold public office. Adding political controversy to his religious problems, in an effort to influence the Parliamentary elections of 1688 he disenfranchised those municipal organizations and other local representative bodies which had previously exercised the power to elect members of the House of Commons.

Matters reached a head in the summer of that year when the queen had a son, James Edward Stuart, whom it was naturally assumed would be raised a Catholic. Prominent politicians decided to act,

A lost cause – James II of England & VII of Scotland leaves for exile in France after the battle of the Boyne. It would take the crushing of two further rebellions for the Hanoverian line to become the undisputed British monarchs. (Art Archive/Tate Gallery)

inviting William of Orange, unswervingly Protestant and an enemy of the French, to assume the throne of Great Britain. Though a foreigner, sound reasons existed for the choice, since William was not only the king's nephew but also his son-in-law, as a consequence of his marriage to Mary, James's daughter. William's supporters hoped this might influence James to alter his policies, though it did not escape them that the Dutch king might accept their proposal as a cynical ploy to depose James, whose friendship with Louis XIV of France naturally caused great concern in Britain. From William's perspective, his dual control of both Britain and the Netherlands would bolster the independence of his homeland, by enabling him to lead a grand coalition against France and stymie Louis XIV's imperial designs. The political and religious rights of people in Britain were therefore hardly foremost in William's calculations; rather, he arrived in England in November 1688 at the head of 14,000 men with the intention of creating a barrier to French territorial ambitions.

James did not lack the personal resolve to resist an invasion, but widespread defections from his army, notably including prominent officers like John Churchill, the future Duke of Marlborough, deprived him of the support necessary to retain his throne in England. Revolts rapidly sprang up across the country in support of William. James tried to negotiate but failed to make progress, whereupon he fled to France in December 1688 and sought the protection of Louis XIV.

With William now ensconced in power, Parliamentary elections took place in England in January 1689. This body passed the Declaration of Rights, which set limits to monarchical rule whereby the king could no longer rule absolutely in the manner of his predecessor. In short, the exercise of power now depended on the consent of a freely elected legislature, which could limit the king's prerogative respecting such issues as the suspension of law, the levying of taxation and the maintenance of a standing army in peacetime. To these restrictions

William willingly consented when he assumed the throne as king (with his wife Mary as queen). In the event, the king's subsequent relationship with Parliament assumed a difficult aspect, for he often tested the boundaries of his authority, which at times extended to the realms of arbitrary rule so characteristic of the previous reign. While Parliament had no wish to relinquish its new-found rights and staunchly resisted the extension of royal power, this political wrangling never reached an intensity sufficient to unleash a strong Jacobite reaction in England until well after William's death; not, in fact, until the accession of George I in 1714.

In Ireland, however, William faced a direct threat when in March 1689 James landed and received immediate local support from Richard Talbot, the Earl of Tyrconnell, who had continued to administer the country as Lord Deputy in James's stead, William not having gained full control over the island. Thus, Ireland, a country divided by religion owing to the settlement of Protestant Lowland Scots in Ulster over the previous hundred years, became a battleground between William and James. It reached a crescendo at the battle of the Boyne in July 1690, though this by no means marked the end of the conflict in Ulster, which continued for another year.

The terms of the Treaty of Limerick, which ended the war in 1691, allowed thousands of Irish Catholics in James's army to go into exile. Most of these were native Irishmen, with many officers from the Catholic gentry who could trace their origins to the era before Protestants established the plantations in the north. Others who served James were of English stock, their forebears having settled in Ireland centuries before. Not content to remain in an Ireland under a Protestant Ascendancy, they chose instead to enter the army of Louis XIV, forming a unit of exiles called the Irish Brigade. Many such exiles settled in other Catholic countries in Europe, establishing themselves in trade and business. Together with English and many Scottish Catholic exiles, they constituted a

John Graham of Claverhouse, Viscount Dundee, who raised the Jacobite standard on behalf of James II & VII in April 1689. Although his forces badly defeated government troops at Killiecrankie, he himself was killed at their head (shown here), depriving the cause of a charismatic leader. (Mary Evans Picture Library)

large community of Jacobite supporters in Europe. Disparate but by no means inconsequential, they would survive as a political force into the mid-18th century and help keep alive the flame of Jacobitism. Of all James' supporters, however, the Jacobite community in Scotland remained the most important to his hope of regaining the crown.

Nevertheless, circumstances in Scotland bore little resemblance to those in Ireland and on the Continent, for many Scots accused James of abusing his position as king, exercising power in an arbitrary manner and subverting the constitutional rights of his people. A stern reaction followed: Catholics were barred from public office, and the episcopacy condemned. In the winter of 1688–89 200 Episcopalian ministers – many, but by no means all, Jacobite sympathizers – were forcibly expelled from their positions, mostly in the Presbyterian stronghold of the south-west. More clergy refused to withdraw their oaths of allegiance to James in favour of William and Mary; they too were expelled, becoming known as 'non-juring' Episcopalians. Despite this persecution, the Episcopalian Church maintained support across the Highlands, particularly among the clans in the north-east of the country, whereas Presbyterianism was largely limited to a few clans like the Campbells, headed by the Earls of Argyll, and the Gordons, under the Earls of Sutherland.

In the summer of 1690 William reluctantly restored Presbyterian government to the national Church, on the basis that the Scots Parliament would otherwise refuse him the funds he desperately required to wage the war which had broken out with France the previous year, and which had resulted in the failed French expedition to Ireland in support of James. A meeting of the Church's General Assembly took place in October 1690, but only 180 ministers and elders attended (although almost 1,000 parishes existed in Scotland). These were mostly from the Lowlands, and included many who had lost their positions in the 1660s during the reign of Charles II for refusing to accept the Episcopalian Church. The Assembly effectively began the purge of Episcopalianism – a process which in the end took decades – while in the meantime Presbyterianism survived quite strongly in the Scottish Lowlands, with qualified support offered first to William, then Queen Anne and later the Hanoverian line. At the same time, Episcopalianism carried on in the north of Scotland, adhered to not only by the Highland clans but also in some areas of the Lowlands, such as those in the north-east around Aberdeen.

The Jacobites were almost entirely committed Episcopalians, with the remainder belonging to the minority Catholic community, and their cause came to be associated with the non-juring Episcopalians. Quite apart from their religious sensibilities, it was on a purely

The Glencoe Massacre, 13 February 1692. Following the rebellion of 1689, King William offered to pardon all chiefs who swore an oath of allegiance to him by the beginning of 1692. Notwithstanding the submission of Alisdair Maclain, chief of the (Jacobite) MacDonalds of Glencoe, two companies of the Duke of Argyll's Regiment shot and bayoneted 38 clansmen near Fort William in an atrocity which lived on in popular Scottish imagination for generations. (Mary Evans Picture Library)

political level that the great majority of Episcopalians adhered to the Jacobite cause, persuaded as they were that the Stuarts were entitled to rule Scotland by divine right. On this basis, therefore, the country stood divided, with potential conflict ever-present.

When William and Mary ascended the throne, the principal Scottish political figures largely accepted the situation, although John Graham of Claverhouse, whom James II & VII had created Viscount Dundee, refused to recognize the new sovereign and led a revolt on behalf of the deposed Scottish king in April 1689. It was to be the first of three Jacobite revolts, and began a few weeks after James had landed in Ireland. He achieved initial success at the battle of Killiecrankie on 27 July, but he was killed there, and without his exceptional leadership the rebellion began to founder, though ultimate defeat did not occur until the decisive battle of Cromdale on 1 May 1690.

In an attempt to pacify the Jacobite clans, John Campbell of Glenorchy, first Earl of Breadalbane, ordered the clan chiefs to submit to the government, or face outlawing. But the clan chiefs insisted their submission would not be forthcoming until the exiled James, residing in France, gave his consent. After months of delay, this consent arrived just before the expiration of the government's deadline of 31 December 1691. Alasdair Maclain, the chief of the MacDonalds of Glencoe, was unable to formally submit before the deadline, and Sir John Dalrymple of Stair, the Secretary of State for Scotland and a rival of Breadalbane, used the delay as a pretext for launching a punitive expedition against the clan.

The troops who would conduct what became known as the Glencoe Massacre consisted of Campbell soldiers from the Duke of Argyll's Regiment – a clan loyal to the government, but also long-standing rivals of the MacDonalds – to give the

John Campbell, 2nd Duke of Argyll. Chief of Clan Campbell and commander of government forces at Sheriffmuir in 1715, Argyll had served under the Duke of Marlborough in the War of the Spanish Succession at the battles of Ramillies, Oudenarde and Malplaquet. He became a field marshal in 1736 and served briefly as commander-in-chief of the British Army in 1742 until his death the following year. (Virginia Historical Society, Richmond/The Bridgeman Art Library)

appearance of an act of revenge against a rival clan. Yet this was not the case. Dalrymple, who had served under James II & VII, was motivated by a desire to demonstrate his loyalty to the new sovereign and, in any event, deeply despised the Highland clans. The Glencoe Massacre served Jacobite propaganda well, for across the country the public were horrified by the atrocity and William had signed the orders that authorized it. The enquiry that followed proved a whitewash, with the king seeking to protect himself from implication, leaving Dalrymple to take the blame and resign from office.

Although the Jacobite cause would derive most of its strength from its Scottish supporters, and the image of the 1745 Rebellion is indelibly that of a Highland

revolt, in 17th- and 18th-century Scotland the allegiances of the clans were divided between Hanoverian and Jacobite, their loyalties driven by politics, economics and religion. Those clans which adhered to religious faiths considered suspect by dint of their ostensible connection with Jacobitism; those which rejected the Hanoverians as upstarts bent on breaking the traditional feudal ties of Highland life; those who rejected the Act of Union or who for any of a host of reasons looked to the House of Stuart as their true sovereign – these clans almost inevitably supported the Jacobite cause either overtly by supplying troops and funds, or by their refusal to aid government efforts at suppressing it. Those clans, Highland and Lowland, which viewed the government and Crown in London as the essential bedrock upon which rested their authority, economic livelihoods and political futures within a united kingdom, naturally sided with the Hanoverian establishment.

Conflict with France was also destined to affect Scottish affairs, for when the Nine Years' War was ended in 1697 by the Treaty of Ryswyck, Louis XIV recognized William as King of Great Britain, and so ended for the moment the possibility of French help for James's restoration. Nevertheless the chance of a peaceful Stuart restoration was less remote than circumstances suggested. William offered the throne to James II & VII's son, James Edward Stuart, his recognized heir, so long as William could continue to rule without interference until his death and so long as the exiled king would raise James Edward a Protestant. As James adamantly refused to consider this proposition, the throne would by right pass to Princess Anne, the younger sister of William's wife, Mary. William offered the same terms again in 1700, after the death of Anne's last surviving son, but James again refused.

Thereafter no Catholic claimant could reach the throne, for in 1701 the English Parliament passed the Act of Settlement, restricting the sovereign to Protestantism in general, and Anglicanism in particular. The Act abolished the rights of all 57 claimants to the throne who were descended by whatever connection to James VI of Scotland. Instead, in the likely event that William and Princess Anne died without heirs, it guaranteed the succession to a granddaughter of James: Sophia, Electress of Hanover, and her descendants. This proved the case, and thus by this Act, following Anne's reign (1702–14), Sophia's son George, Elector of Hanover, became King of Great Britain as George I, so inaugurating the Hanoverian line that reigned on the British throne until Victoria's accession in 1837. Significantly, the English Parliament passed this legislation without any discussion with its Scottish counterpart – which had itself proposed nothing of the kind – thereby generating considerable ill-feeling over a matter with far-reaching constitutional implications.

Further rebuffs and offence to the Scots Parliament occurred in 1702, when the English Parliament declared war on France without any consultation with its counterpart in Edinburgh. This new conflict, the War of the Spanish Succession, was an international power struggle resulting from the absence of a Bourbon heir on the death of Charles II of Spain in 1700, and pitted a Protestant alliance consisting of Britain, the Netherlands and the Holy Roman Empire (a loose-knit body of western and central German states) against Catholic France and Spain. The year previously James II & VII had died, and so by this point James Francis Edward Stuart, later to become known as the 'Old Pretender', had already succeeded him as Stuart claimant to the throne.

The Act of Settlement contributed strongly to the series of events which led to the Act of Union between England and Scotland, which elicited no small degree of resentment amongst the Scottish populace and, above all, the Jacobites. Determined not to concede its ancient rights, in 1703 the Scots Parliament passed the Act of Security, under the terms of which the Hanoverian line were only to be entitled to the Crown of Scotland if the Westminster Parliament recognized the sovereignty of the Parliament

Prince James Francis Edward Stuart. Known as the 'Old Pretender', he lacked the energy and enthusiasm of his elder son, Charles, and earned the nickname 'Old Mister Melancholy'. (Scottish National Portrait Gallery, Edinburgh/The Bridgeman Art Library)

in Edinburgh. In fact, the Act specifically guaranteed the sovereignty of the crown and kingdom of Scotland, the independence of its Parliament, its religion, and the protection of the country's trade from English influence. The Act also required all Protestant men old enough to serve in the militia to receive training in defence of the kingdom, which implied that Scotland was prepared to fight against English encroachments on its liberties. A further Act stipulated that whoever succeeded Queen Anne could not declare war without in the first instance consulting the Scots Parliament.

The English Parliament took umbrage at this expression of defiance and recommended that the Queen order troops to the border, that the militia be called out in the northern counties of England and further troops sent to Carlisle, Berwick and Newcastle – all within easy striking distance of Scotland. Anglo–Scottish relations

John Erskine, sixth Earl of Mar. He served as Secretary of State for Scotland under the Tory ministry during Queen Anne's reign, but when George I assumed the throne on her death, Mar found himself dismissed from government service, after which he raised the Jacobite standard for James Edward Stuart in 1715. (Author's collection)

deteriorated further in February 1705 when Westminster passed the Alien Act, which demanded that by Christmas of that year the Scots Parliament repeal the 1703 Act of Security – thereby accepting the Hanoverian succession unconditionally – or enter discussions for the union of the respective countries' Parliaments. Failing this, all Scots living outside of England would be regarded as foreigners and all Scottish imports refused entry across the border. This economic threat proved grave indeed, for the principal landowners in Scotland, far beyond merely the nobility alone, depended heavily upon the export of their coal, cattle and linen to England. To them, union with England appeared to be at the very least an economic necessity, for without access to England's colonial trade, much of it managed by the monopolistic East India Company, Scotland's prosperity would suffer. There seemed virtually no prospect of Scotland carving out an empire or colonial markets of its own after a disastrous attempt to settle a colony in Central America had failed in 1698.

The Scots Parliament naturally debated the Act of Union, but the commissioners appointed to do so were nominated by Queen Anne, and thus enjoyed little credibility among Scots. Nevertheless, the Act of Union was passed by the Scottish Parliament on 16 January 1707, and it gave birth to the new political entity of 'Great Britain' with a single parliament in London – to the accompaniments of riots in Edinburgh, Glasgow and other cities. Even where opposition was peaceful, there was general discontent at the fact that the commissioners rejected the preferred federal compromise, by which Scotland could maintain its independence as a nation. As union affected religious as well as political issues – for by it Presbyterianism became the national Church of Scotland – the abolition of Scottish independence numbered amongst a growing list of grievances harboured by those still committed to the return of the Stuart dynasty. Before he died James II & VII had told his son never to accept a union between Scotland and England, and thus the repeal of the Act of Union stood high amongst Jacobite aspirations.

Louis XIV appreciated that popular dissatisfaction with the Act of Union offered a strategic opportunity while he remained at war with Britain, if he could profit by Jacobite frustrations and restore the Stuart dynasty with the aid of French troops. Thus, in 1708 he ordered the assembly of a naval expedition which was to transport James Edward Stuart to Scotland. Five ships of the line and 20 other vessels sailed from Dunkirk in March, carrying 5,000 French troops and enough weapons for 13,000 men. The fleet encountered stormy seas and overshot the landing point, ultimately anchoring off Crail at the mouth of the Forth. A reconnaissance force went ashore, but when it encountered only a small group of Jacobite supporters the French commanders refused to land the Prince despite his strenuous protests, correctly deducing the exaggerated nature of James' claim that the whole country would rise in his support. The following morning a running action took place between rival French and British fleets, obliging the French to proceed north – so far, in fact, as to bring them entirely around the north coast of Scotland and back to Dunkirk, in the process losing several ships to adverse weather west of Ireland.

The expedition was a total failure, but failure might very well have been the outcome even if the Prince had landed and proclaimed a free Parliament as he intended, together with a call for a constitution and discussions to establish a new national church. The fact remained that, at least in the Lowlands, the population benefited from the 1707 Act of Union, which amongst many other principles guaranteed the existence of the Presbyterian Church as Scotland's established faith. South of the river Tay, Scotland could be relied upon not to back a Catholic monarch imposing himself on this Protestant country, whatever

reforms James proposed to implement once on the throne. Many of the great landowners were similarly disinclined to support the Jacobite cause, for most had supported the Act of Union only the previous year.

After his return to France in 1708, James Edward Stuart served Louis XIV as a military commander, participating in the battles of Oudenarde and Malplaquet (1708 and 1709 respectively), fighting troops whom – ironically – he claimed as his subjects. The war ended with the Treaty of Utrecht in July 1713, whose terms obliged France to no longer allow the Prince protection on French

The Earl of Mar raising the Old Pretender's standard at Braemar, September 1715. The Jacobites quickly took Inverness and Perth but failed to occupy Edinburgh. Rebel strength rose rapidly: by early October Mar had 5,000 infantry and 1,000 cavalry, with 2,500 Highlanders from the western clans marching to join him. More than 3,000 were gathering in the north of Scotland as well. (The Stapleton Collection/The Bridgeman Art Library)

The battle of Sheriffmuir, 13 November 1715. The Duke of Argyll, with 900 cavalry and 2,200 infantry confronted the Earl of Mar's 900 horse and 6,200 foot east of Dunblane. In bizarre fashion, Mar's right wing routed Argyll's left just before Argyll's cavalry drove off the victorious attackers. Both sides then reformed, but despite Mar's numerical superiority and better ground, he declined to attack. The battle ended indecisively with the onset of darkness. (Art Archive/Private collection)

soil, whereupon he left for Germany. Thereafter Queen Anne refused James's entreaties that he should succeed her as the rightful heir, accepting nothing short of his conversion to Anglicanism, which the Prince flatly refused to contemplate. Anne died on 1 August 1714, whereupon George I became King of Great Britain. A new upsurge of Jacobite grievances led to a serious rebellion the following year, much of it centred on the failure of the Act of Union to bring Scotland the economic benefits that had been promised, together with the government's refusal to extend rights promised to the Scots, and restrictions imposed on the religious freedoms of the established Church of Scotland.

Matters came to a head when the Earl of Mar raised the Prince's standard at Braemar in September 1715. Jacobite forces captured Inverness and Perth but failed to take Edinburgh Castle. By the following month Mar had 6,000 men under arms, with 2,500 clansmen from the west moving to join him, upwards of 3,000 more coming from the north, and small numbers of supporters in the north of England and the Scottish Borders gathering. Meanwhile, the Duke of Argyll, the commander of government forces in Scotland, busied himself increasing the Hanoverian military presence north of the border, although this did not prevent, in late October, the Jacobites from invading England where they expected support from supposed adherents in Lancashire. The rebels duly reached Preston, where government troops under General Wills attacked the town from two directions on 12 November, accepting the surrender of its garrison two days later.

On the 13th, meanwhile, Argyll met Mar's forces at the battle of Sheriffmuir, near Dunblane, which ended indecisively after the approach of darkness. Still, the action denied Mar the ability to move south as he had intended, and with many Highlanders deserting, he returned to Perth. The Earl of Sutherland, meanwhile, with clans loyal to the government, retook Inverness, and in the last months of the year Mar's forces continued to dwindle through desertion while Argyll's increased. Thus, even when James Edward Stuart landed near Aberdeen in late December, the declining

The battle of Glenshiel, 10 June 1719. The decisive, and indeed the only major action of the failed Jacobite rising of 1719, in which 1,100 government troops under General Wightman attacked 1,500 Jacobites and a small contingent of Spanish troops, routing the Highlanders and driving the Spaniards back to a new position, where they surrendered the following day. (Scottish National Portrait Gallery, Edinburgh/The Bridgeman Art Library)

Council held by the Earl of Mar, commander of Jacobite forces in 1715, before the battle of Sheriffmuir. The revolt of 1715 began on a sound military footing, but failed partly because of the absence of a rising in England. (Author's collection)

fortunes of the Jacobite cause were clear for all to see. With the Jacobites in retreat by the end of January 1716, the Prince embarked for France, the loyal clans dispersed to their respective homes, and the rebellion ground to an end by mid-February. For several months government forces remained in the pro-Jacobite areas of Scotland in an effort to stamp out the last vestiges of the rebellion, seizing the property of prominent rebels and disarming clans known to have participated in the uprising or which were suspected of aiding it. The inaccessibility of the Highlands hampered this work, and in the end reprisals fell relatively lightly on the Scots but rather more harshly on those areas of England where Jacobite support was strongest.

Following the collapse of the '15, James did not find himself welcomed on his return to France. Louis XIV was now dead and the Regent no longer wished to pursue the late king's hostile policies against Britain, including providing safe haven to the Hanoverians' enemies. Indeed, the British government had not overlooked the Bourbon record for harbouring and abetting Jacobite leaders and their sympathizers; by the terms of the Treaty of Utrecht which had ended the war in 1714, the French had agreed not to allow James residence on their soil.

Accordingly, he and his retinue of exiled adherents eventually settled in Rome, as guests of the Pope. There the Jacobite cause continued to smoulder, with the movements and cabals of its supporters the focus of considerable attention by British agents on the Continent for the next 30 years. Events soon justified their suspicions. The '15 had demonstrated that the chief potential threat remained a rising among the Jacobite clans in

Scotland, supported by regular troops supplied from the Continent. Only four years later, Philip V of Spain found he could make use of the Jacobites in a disruptive capacity – partly in reprisal for the destruction of the Spanish fleet off Cape Passaro – by launching a diversionary expedition to Scotland and effecting a major landing in England. While the main fleet was defeated at sea the diversionary force, complete with Spanish mercenaries, landed in Scotland to cooperate with Highlanders and Jacobite exiles under the command of the Marquess of Tullibardine, a Scottish Jacobite returned from exile. When his forces met General Wightman's government troops at Glenshiel on the west coast on 10 June 1719, they were driven from the field, the Highlanders evaporating into the glens beyond the reach of the authorities and leaving the Spanish to capture and eventual repatriation. James learned of the disaster while in Madrid and thereafter took no further active part in attempting to restore his dynasty to the British throne – except perhaps in one way. In September he married a Polish noblewoman who the following year bore him a son, Prince Charles Edward Stuart. Twenty-four years later, it would be this young man, Bonnie Prince Charlie, who would launch the last major attempt to re-establish the Stuart dynasty on the British throne.

The armies of two kings

The British Army

The elements of the British Army that fought in the campaigns of 1745–46 were of mixed quality, from units comprised of raw recruits to veteran regiments recalled from the Continent where they were engaged with the French in the War of the Austrian Succession (1740–48). The public viewed the Army with suspicion, as memories of Cromwell's employment of troops under the Commonwealth to maintain his hold over the nation and quash Parliament remained fixed in the British imagination, which, taking a jaundiced view, regarded a standing army more as an instrument of tyranny and an unnecessary public expense than a vital instrument for the nation's defence.

Regiments were comprised of one or in some cases two battalions (which, it must be stressed, almost never operated in the field together or indeed even served in the same campaign) with each battalion consisting of ten companies of about 30 to 40 officers and men, giving a full unit strength of between 300 and 400 of all ranks. Each regiment bore both a number and the name of its colonel, though such officers seldom accompanied their regiments, the responsibility for administration in the field falling to the lieutenant-colonel or the major. Since a regiment seldom fielded more than one battalion, 'regiment' and 'battalion' became effectively synonymous terms.

The infantry carried a heavy, hard-wearing muzzle-loading smooth-bore flintlock musket which fired a round lead ball weighing just over an ounce. A trained infantryman could fire at a rate of two rounds a minute, supported in close combat by his 17-inch steel bayonet, though it must be emphasized that the outcome of battle in the 18th century depended much more heavily on the effectiveness of small-arms fire than on hand-to-hand fighting. In action, the battalion deployed in three-rank lines in order to bring the maximum number of muskets to bear. Firing by platoon, if performed correctly, enabled the unit to discharge its weapons in a continuous fashion. Over time and amidst the pressure of battle, platoon-firing sometimes degenerated into a continuous, uncoordinated fusillade, but so long as the distance to the enemy stood at less than 100 yards – or ideally closer to half that distance – the infantry could achieve an effective and quite often devastating result.

A British officer during the 1745 Rebellion. As a body officers could hardly be described as implacable enemies of Jacobitism – but being sworn to defend the Crown they prosecuted the campaign with at least as much vigour as that shown against the French. (National Army Museum)

Hogarth's depiction of the Guards marching to Scotland. At the outbreak of the rebellion virtually the whole of the British Army was already engaged on the Continent against the French and could offer only limited resistance to rising Jacobite fortunes. Even after Cumberland's forces returned home, amidst the Jacobite invasion of England, the rebels managed to elude him and might well have reached London, thus dramatically changing the course of the conflict. (National Army Museum)

Cavalry played a relatively minor role in the rebellion, except at Culloden, where Cumberland deployed two regiments of dragoons and one of light horse. Dragoons, originally operating as mounted infantry but infrequently used for this purpose, wielded a straight, heavy broadsword similar to that carried by Highlanders, two pistols and a shorter version of the infantry musket for use on foot. Regiments of light horse wielded a curved sabre, two pistols and a carbine – a lighter and smaller-calibre weapon than the musket carried by dragoons – which could be employed in the saddle. Regiments were divided into squadrons and further into troops, with units seldom numbering more than 200–300 of all ranks – at best qualifying as an understrength regiment. Cavalry charged with drawn sword, but only at the trot; they never reached the gallop as would become customary later in the century.

The Army deployed only a handful of guns in the rebellion, and only made effective use of these at Culloden, where Cumberland employed six mortars and ten 3-pounder cannons (to the Army, always 'guns'), whose shot bounded across the ground, mangling those unfortunate enough to stand in their path. Mortars fired a type of explosive shell dependent for its effectiveness both on proper trajectory and a well-timed fuse. Rounds lobbed indirectly over walls and fences offered unreliable results unless handled by a well-trained crew.

Most soldiers were drawn from the ranks of agricultural labourers and those who had conducted a trade such as shoe-making, carpentry or cloth-making, and accepted the king's shilling if they fell on hard times. Thus, the stereotypical characterization of the army as a reservoir of criminality – men coerced into service as an alternative to prison – is not entirely borne out by the facts. Most recruits were young, between 17 and 25, though as service was for life, or until such time as infirmity rendered them no longer fit and useful as soldiers, it was not uncommon to find men in their thirties or even forties still serving. Still, the emergency created by the rebellion led the government to pass Acts in rapid succession to meet the immediate need for more troops. Such Acts amounted to something akin to what the Navy practised by the name of impressment; that is, forcible enlistment, although never in substantial numbers. Under these Acts, the authorities leant on magistrates to make available to the Army all 'able-bodied men who do not follow or exercise any lawful calling or employment', as well as 'all such able-bodied, idle and disorderly persons who cannot upon examination prove themselves to exercise and industriously follow some lawful trade or employment, or to have some substance sufficient for their support and maintenance'. The soldiers enlisted by this method rarely possessed prior military experience, and consequently found themselves performing non-combat tasks.

Officers, though socially far more diverse than popularly believed, generally sprang from the upper middle class, the landed gentry and the aristocracy. Senior officers, in particular, largely attained their rank through patronage – connections with prominent members of the Army or the government. In addition to influence, wealth played a prominent part; since promotion arose almost exclusively through purchase of commissions, those with money necessarily dominated the officer corps. Those junior officers with more limited opportunities for promotion tended to derive from the less exalted sphere of the middle class, but nonetheless bore by their position the distinction of 'gentleman', being often the sons of officers themselves, or of physicians, ministers or tradesmen of comfortable means. Of course, a small number of men became officers by virtue

of promotion from the ranks in recognition for distinguished service, but these formed a distinct minority.

British infantry were highly adept at musketry, the result of the great emphasis placed on small-arms drill. In most other respects training was sometimes woefully inadequate, though to be fair this varied according to the individual merits of the regimental commander, as no uniformity of training – or even regulations governing its frequency – yet existed in the Army. As James Wolfe, the future commander of the force that took Quebec in 1759, observed:

I have but a very mean opinion of the infantry in general. I know their discipline to be bad, & their valour precarious. They are easily put into disorder, & hard to recover out of it; they frequently kill their Officers thro' fear & murder one another in their confusion...

The loyalist Highlanders

Amongst the numerous clans spread widely across the Highlands and islands, it was Clan Campbell that exercised the most powerful influence in the west of Scotland, especially in Argyll, under the duke of that name. Still other branches of Campbells lived under the feudal influence of the earls of Breadalbane, Loudoun, and various lesser chiefs, and in 1745, it was John Campbell, Earl of Loudoun, who commanded all loyalist independent companies and the more informally organized clan recruits.

While the Campbell leadership itself stood loyal to King George, ordinary clansmen probably held no special place in their hearts for this 'German' sovereign, and served their chiefs during the rebellion only out of loyalty and obligation – in the same manner as many of their Jacobite counterparts, by no means all of whom embraced the notion of a Stuart restoration. Thus, to many of both the loyalist and rebel rank-and-file clansmen, the '45 represented a clash between rival clans – albeit on a large scale – providing in the case of the Campbells an opportunity to avenge past and present wrongs against the MacLeans,

Highlanders firing from an elevated position. One of the chief weaknesses of the clansmen's otherwise fine martial skills was their impetuous character and lack of knowledge in the proper use of firearms. (Mary Evans Picture Library)

Camerons and the Stewarts of Appin, against all of whom the Campbells harboured long-standing grievances of one kind or another, many avenged by cattle-raiding forays or violence, only to be returned in kind in a vicious cycle sometimes stretching back generations.

Various loyalist units supported the Government, most prominently the Duke of Argyll's Regiment, a militia whose tradition of service to the Protestant line dated back to 1689 and its establishment under William and Mary. The Duke of Argyll's Regiment was raised from the clansmen and tenantry of the aristocracy of Argyll, Loudoun and Breadalbane, and its men were mostly volunteers from Clan Campbell. Their colonel was the son of John Campbell of Mamore, a major-general of Argyll Militia, a loyal supporter of the government and a kinsman of the Duke of Argyll, hence the unit's designation. The independent companies raised by Lord President Forbes in the northern and western Highlands accounted for most of the men furnished by the loyal clans. Poorly trained and seldom particularly motivated, they proved an indifferent presence in battle – which often accounted

for their odd deployment. The Argyll Militia, which boasted 12 companies at the battle of Falkirk, were posted on the far right, near the bottom of the hill. In the same action, the Glasgow Militia, being considered insufficiently trained to be fit for the line, were placed on the hill but behind a line of dragoons. Still, when decently officered and in the presence of regular troops, loyalist militia could perform well, as did the eight companies of Argylls at Culloden, where they pursued the fleeing Camerons and appear also to have accelerated from the field the retreating Royal Scots under Lord John Drummond. The Campbells, like their rebel counterparts, wore the kilt, dirk, plaid, musket and broadsword, but to distinguish themselves as loyal to the Hanoverian line wore in their dark bonnets a badge of myrtle and a red or yellow saltire, as opposed to the white ribbon or cockade of the Jacobites.

The Jacobite army

As is well known, the Jacobites drew the bulk of their forces from the Highlands, but the clansmen's motives for participation in the rebellion widely varied. Some joined out of a mere sense of duty to their chief or landlord, and those whose hearts did not truly rest in the cause sometimes made indifferent fighters. Others, compelled to serve by threats made against themselves or their families and with the prospect of seeing their house burned and their cattle driven off, joined the Prince's army with even less enthusiasm than those motivated by fealty. Nevertheless, if an element of coercion existed in the Jacobites' recruitment policies, plenty of men qualified as genuine volunteers; on the whole these men endured the trials of campaigning and

Senior officer of a Highland regiment. The motivations of such men had less to do with wreaking vengeance on hereditary foes – though this cannot be altogether discounted – by seizing their cattle and land, but more to do with improving conditions in their communities and, on a grander scale, separating the English and Scottish crowns. (Stuart Reid collection)

battle with considerably more resilience and fortitude than those who simply enlisted by virtue of carrot or stick. These men, possessing genuine faith in the righteousness of their cause and manifesting a strong personal attachment to the Prince, were the most likely to serve as officers and cavalrymen – and played the most prominent parts in battle.

A fair number came from the ranks of the British Army as deserters, often taken as prisoners and agreeing to fight for the Jacobites, though as few appear to have figured amongst the captives after Culloden it is likely that their motives for serving the Prince amounted to little more than an opportunity to avoid captivity. Following that disastrous battle, most of them left the Jacobite ranks in search of more reliable employment, such as in the French regiments that had been serving in the Jacobite army – exile units like the Irish Picquets and the Royal Ecossois, the latter a Scottish regiment in the service of Louis XV.

Highlanders alone did not account for the whole of the Jacobite forces; men drawn from the Scottish Lowlands in the role of fencibles or militia also joined up, with recruiters requiring landowners to supply either a quota of men or a sum of money in lieu. As in the Highlands, Jacobite commanders in the Lowlands sometimes employed terror, such as farm burning, to compel men to 'come out'. Apart from volunteers and impressed men, an unknown number of men joined the ranks as mercenaries. It is worth noting that total clan strength ran to at least 32,000 men (albeit including the loyalist clans), and yet perhaps only 6,000 men turned out in favour of the Young Pretender.

The Jacobite army contained a disproportionate number of officers, for commissions were issued to just about anyone whose social status appeared to qualify him as a gentleman. To some extent the authorities solved this problem by amalgamating some of the many smaller formations to bring them up to a respectable strength (there existed no conventional size for Jacobite regiments; instead, many were formed simply on the basis of the relationship between the men and a particular commander or clan). In the end, however, it was not uncommon for senior officers to lead 'regiments' whose numbers qualified them only as independent companies. Such officers, though perhaps capable as managers of farms or small businesses and of unquestioned bravery in battle, could not necessarily meet the demands that are placed on the leaders of bodies of armed men; this resulted in Jacobite units on campaign sometimes displaying a lack of professional efficiency in such matters as the issuing and fulfilling of orders. If such men showed no hesitation in leading their men in the charge, they were as a rule not so adept in training or instilling discipline; although some attempts were made to teach their men drill and musketry, officers did so without the advice and support of properly experienced NCOs.

For the most part Jacobite infantry wore a more-or-less consistent style of dress, details of which Wade had described 20 years before the rebellion during his visit to the Highlands:

The Arms they make use of in War, are a Musket, a Broad Sword and a Target [a wooden shield], a Pistol and a Durk [a type of long knife] or Dagger, hanging by their side, with a Powder Horn and Pouch for their Ammunition. They form themselves into Bodies of unequal Numbers according to the Strength of their Clan or Tribe which is Commanded by their Respective Superior or Chieftain.

On the other hand, the weapons recovered by government troops from Jacobite prisoners at Culloden do not appear to support the view, popular among filmmakers and novelists, that every man carried such a full range of weaponry, though it is fair to say that he was generally well-clothed and identifiable by clan according to his distinctive plaid. In reality, no more than a third of clansman appear to have carried a broadsword, but those who did – generally men of higher social status – occupied the

A Highlander. Clansmen were variously armed – by no means all with broadswords as popular sentiment suggests. The poorest men carried simple implements like pitchforks and scythes, while others carried Lochaber axes (a type of polearm) or muskets. (Stuart Reid collection)

front rank in battle, with their dependents arrayed behind with muskets and bayonets, mostly of Continental manufacture. Many of these the French had landed at Montrose and Peterhead, though some the rebels captured after battle, at Prestonpans and elsewhere.

Jacobite infantry tactics varied from the Lowlanders' adaptations of French methods, which called for a four-deep fighting formation which emphasized the use of the bayonet over musketry, to the classic Highland way of war: a rapid advance on the enemy with little concern for dressing the ranks or keeping some sort of organized formation. This was consistent with centuries of tradition and, in any event, in the absence of orthodox military training or discipline any other method was out of the question. Once in close proximity to the enemy line, the Highlanders discharged their firearms before continuing forwards at a run, amidst ferocious cries and with swords held aloft, through the smoke and into the ranks of the opposing line, where combat with hand weapons finished the business. The Highlanders' charge took the form of a compact column or wedge, with the swordsmen invariably occupying the front rank.

As the Highlanders offered no genuine preparatory fire, the success of their charge depended entirely on the expectation of the receiving troops collapsing in the mêlée that followed the onslaught of a howling, sword-wielding throng of opponents, which after a brief clash of steel would instigate panic and a rout. If, however, the defending infantry maintained their composure and fired in disciplined volleys in the manner instilled in them by incessant drill, they stood a reasonable chance of fending off their attackers with the bayonet once the dreaded and inevitable collision occurred.

Therein lay the problem for the Highlanders. Success against well-drilled, disciplined troops depended heavily on psychology and intimidation – producing such trepidation in the hearts of the defender that his nerve failed him, so allowing the sheer weight and ferocity of the charge to shatter both the enemy's morale and his unit integrity. This was all very well against unsteady or poorly trained troops, but against professionals it left something to be desired. As Lord George Murray, commander of the Jacobite forces, learned from his subordinates after Falkirk, unless the Highlanders

... could attack the enemy at very considerable advantage, either by surprise or by some strong situation of ground, or a narrow pass, they could not expect any great success, especially if their numbers were no ways equal,

and that a body of regular troops was absolutely necessary to support them, when they should at any time go in, sword in hand; for they were sensible, that without more leisure and time to discipline their own men, it would not be possible to make them keep their ranks, or rally soon enough upon any sudden emergency, so that any small number of the enemy, either keeping in a body [i.e. a reserve] when they were in confusion, or rallying, would deprive them of a victory, even after they had done their best.

Regimental commanders clearly appreciated that despite the bravery of their men, their unconventional tactics and system of loose discipline demanded reform; in the short term, the army also needed a stiffening of regulars – the implication being that these would be French units.

Jacobite cavalry, in the form of such irregular units as Lord Pitsligo's Horse, Fitzjames' Horse and Lord Kilmarnock's Horse Grenadiers, played only a minor role in the conflict. The absence of formal training and its small numbers left the cavalry with no pretensions to being the equal of its regular counterparts in the British Army, but it did prove its utility in reconnaissance. Cavalry officers ranged from titled gentlemen from Edinburgh and other urban areas, to wealthy merchants and small property-owners (or their sons), with the ranks filled by the lesser-born. The Jacobite horse performed well on patrol, though they were prone to looting. Apart from the requisite sword, most troopers carried a musket.

Jacobite artillery, of varied calibre and largely consisting of light-calibre pieces captured from the British Army plus a few pieces supplied by the French from guns captured at the battle of Fontenoy, played a small part in operations and generally performed poorly in the hands of undermanned and virtually untrained crews.

The Bonnie Prince's rebellion

If there was a lesson to be derived from the rebellion of 1715 it was that there could be no hope of success without external assistance, whether this assumed the guise of foreign troops, arms and money, or volunteers from across England. But if the '15 had failed, the hopes and dreams of Jacobites had been far from extinguished. Despite the dissolution of their forces, they had not been vanquished in battle. Thus, the notion of restoring the Stuarts to the throne remained their principal aspiration, only awaiting a more propitious moment before fighting resumed.

Having said this, internal affairs in Britain remained peaceful for the remainder of George I's reign, which ended on his death in 1727, and the premiership under

King George II, whose Hanoverian line did not command universal popularity across Britain – thus giving hope to the Jacobites for support not merely in the Scottish Highlands, but across England. (Art Archive/Handel Museum Halle/Alfredo Dagli Orti)

Sir Robert Walpole managed domestic matters deftly enough to placate Jacobite grievances. With Britain maintaining neutrality in European affairs for over 20 years, the Jacobites could also look to nothing more than moral support from France. Matters shifted in their favour, however, when in 1739 Britain became embroiled in a conflict with Spain known as the War of Jenkins' Ear over the question of the slave trade. The Family Compact between France and Spain – both under Bourbon rule – automatically committed these countries to war if either one opened hostilities with a third. When a general European war began in 1740 owing to Prussia's invasion of Austrian Silesia – with the French as Maria Theresa's ally – Louis XV naturally looked to revive the plan to aid the exiled Stuarts for strategic reasons, this time to divert British attention away from this, the War of the Austrian Succession.

Raising the banner of revolt formed one of the chief topics of discussion between French diplomats in Rome and a host of unofficial Jacobite representatives, who began arriving from Scotland in 1739. Though brought together by common interest, both sides nonetheless looked for assurances from each other; for the Scots, any proposed invasion by the French had to be well supported in material terms, while Paris wished to see a list of names of those Scots and English willing to fight. Jacobite promises that sympathizers in England would rise once an army had taken the field did not sufficiently answer French concern that their troops would be abandoned to their fate, and insisted on a list of supporters.

With Catholic Spain now at war with Britain, Scottish Jacobite and French hopes received a boost, not least when in early 1742 Walpole lost a vote of confidence in the

House of Commons led by Jacobite MPs and dissident Whigs acting on instructions from the Old Pretender. A new ministry, dominated by dissident Whigs, replaced Walpole's administration, with the Secretary of State for Scotland, John Hay, 4th Marquess of Tweeddale, proving indecisive and ineffectual enough to create a vacuum of political power in the Highlands, which Prince Charles Edward eventually discovered he could easily fill. Moreover, in June 1743 when an Anglo-Austrian and Hanoverian army suffered defeat at the hands of the French at Dettingen, Jacobite hopes again rose,

Engagement between the French warship *L'Elisabeth* and HMS *Lion*, 9 July 1745, 100 miles west of Lizard Point. The French frigate *Du Teillay*, carrying the Prince to Scotland, left Nantes on 22 June and on 4 July, off Belle Isle, made a rendezvous with its escort *L'Elisabeth*, which was also loaded with soldiers and arms. Five days later they unexpectedly encountered the 64-gun *Lion*. While the smaller *Du Teillay* largely remained aloof from the action, the *Lion* reduced *L'Elisabeth* to a virtual wreck, though at the cost to herself of most of her rigging. The French ships separated, with *L'Elisabeth* – too damaged to carry on as an escort for the *Du Teillay* – putting back into a French port without even being able to transfer arms or troops to her consort. Undaunted, the Prince determined to carry on and landed on the little island of Eriskay, in the Outer Hebrides, on 23 July. (National Maritime Museum, Greenwich)

whereupon they hatched a plan to send the Old Pretender to Britain. But James Edward Stuart, now in his fifties, declined, instead nominating his son, 'Bonnie Prince Charlie' or the Young Pretender, to lead the revolt. Charles, 24 years old, blessed with remarkable energy and a strong belief in his cause, eagerly accepted the opportunity and happily met the King of France in December 1743 to discuss plans for an expeditionary force. Charles, bidding farewell to his father, left Rome in secret on 9 January 1744, carrying with him authority as regent of Scotland.

His absence from Rome could not go unnoticed for long, particularly by the British agents anxiously watching his movements for signs that would indicate renewed Jacobite activity at home. Charles, travelling in disguise and without the trappings typical of a man of his station, ventured through Tuscany to Savona, where he embarked for the south of France and proceeded by coach to Paris, where he arrived on 29 January. His absence had long since alerted authorities in London, whose anxieties were heightened by the concentration of naval assets in the ports of Dunkirk, Calais and Boulogne. It remains unclear if Charles actually received a royal audience in Paris, but he outlined to

courtiers the prospect of success in very positive terms and emphasized the importance of French troops' participation.

In this regard the king appeared to be true to his word: in November 1743 the king had agreed to dispatch an expedition to Britain, and now 15,000 men were being concentrated at Gravelines for an invasion of Britain at two points, with Marshal de Saxe – one of the best of French commanders – appointed to command the main invasion force. Experience in 1715 had shown that any success would depend partly on the rising of English Jacobites, whom the French must support with a direct military intervention in the south. This was to be provided by a landing in Kent by 12,000 men under de Saxe, with Charles in his train, with the remaining 3,000 men under George Keith, 10th Earl Marischal, descending on Scotland. Any operations which might be expected to move ponderously south from Scotland, even with the expected simultaneous rising, did not suggest themselves as effective; instead, the French planned to execute a rapid

Prince Charles landing at Eriskay, where he took his first steps of the rebellion on Scottish soil. One observer recorded this description of the Prince at Edinburgh: 'The figure and presence of Charles Stuart were not ill suited to his lofty pretensions. He was in the prime of youth, tall and handsome, of a fair complexion; he had a light coloured periwig with his own hair combed over the front; he wore the Highland dress, that is, a tartan short coat without the plaid, a blue bonnet on his head, and on his breast the star of the order of St Andrew.' (Art Archive/Sotheby's)

movement against London with regular troops, ousting the government and king, and placing the Stuarts back in control of the nation's affairs.

The British were not prepared to remain idle while their enemies planned an invasion. Admiral Sir John Norris assumed command of a Channel squadron off Spithead, the government moved troops to the south coast, the Kent militia assembled and troops were withdrawn from active operations against the French in Flanders in order to bolster the defence of southern England. Meanwhile, a French fleet under Admiral Roquefeuille, comprising 22 ships

Prince Charles Edward Stuart. When he raised the standard of revolt in 1745, 56 years had passed since his grandfather had been exiled and three decades since the death of Queen Anne, the last of the Stuart monarchs. (Author's collection)

as an escort for the troop transports meant for the invasion, had already put to sea by the time Charles reached Dunkirk. Norris came within sight of Roquefeuille's fleet on 24 February 1744, whereupon the French admiral, concerned by his opponent's numerical superiority, made sail for France with all haste. Strong winds facilitated his speedy return, but also played havoc with the transports docked in port and awaiting the troops, while other vessels, fully laden, had already embarked. In the event, gales wrecked virtually the entire flotilla, sinking those already at sea and sufficiently damaging those lying in port as to render them unserviceable, with 12 ships foundered and seven lost with all hands. Charles and Marshal de Saxe managed to return safely, but they had only barely escaped.

The vicissitudes of the weather at this point appeared almost providential to the British, for a spy in the French Foreign Ministry confirmed suspicions that an invasion was afoot, prompting the War Office urgently to recall further troops from Flanders and to transfer others from Ireland. The delay caused by the rough weather in the Channel also enabled British authorities to improve their preparations on the south coast of England. Above all, it inflicted such damage on the invasion fleet as to render impossible any imminent invasion.

But despite its failure, its very dispatch had far-reaching implications, for until now Britain and France had remained in contention only on the basis of their alliances with Prussia and Austria, respectively – nations whose armies presently confronted one another in the field. But the hostile intention implied by the assembly of a large fleet and transports in the Channel and the northern French ports now brought Britain and France into open warfare, with formal declarations of war exchanged in October 1744. Under these circumstances, quite apart from the state of France's naval affairs, their troops would now be required to take on the Prussians, whose successes against the Austrians could not go unchallenged. But they also engaged Allied forces in the Austrian Netherlands (Flanders), an area of vital strategic interest to Britain. Thus, with its troops heavily committed on the Continent, in the short term at least France could only offer limited aid to any proposed Jacobite rising across the Channel.

All this put Charles in a difficult situation, for instead of arriving in England with French troops in support of his cause, he remained in France with no material support. Even his presence in Paris did not renew French interest in the cancelled expedition. Matters appeared to turn in the Prince's favour, however, when on 30 April 1745 the French inflicted a serious defeat on the British, Dutch, Austrian and Hanoverian troops at Fontenoy, in the Austrian Netherlands. The commander happened to be the Duke of Cumberland, second son of George II, and with British forces in Flanders performing badly and the country bereft of sufficient forces to mount an adequate defence, now appeared to be the time for the Prince to act.

Fontenoy provided a helpful boost to the Jacobite cause, improving morale and encouraging those who believed that such a victory could be attained on British soil. Fontenoy also obliged King George to keep troops on the Continent, not least when in the wake of the battle the French captured the towns of Tournai, Ghent, Bruges and Ostend. Charles was ebullient, notwithstanding the knowledge, as he had been warned the previous year by one of his prominent adherents, that the Highlanders would not rally round him unless he arrived in Scotland with a large army and sufficient arms to supply his followers. Charles, bent on returning to Scotland whatever the state of feeling in the country, decided to ignore this warning. Having come this far, he would not allow the opportunity to pass while his star appeared to be in the ascendant.

The French, unable to support the Prince with troops or weapons, therefore left him to pursue his own course insofar as he could purchase supplies and vessels at his own expense and leave for Scotland via a French port. Antoine Walsh, a shipowner and Jacobite supporter, provided a vessel, which took aboard approximately 1,500 muskets, 1,800 broadswords, 20 pieces of artillery and a supply of powder and ball, together with several thousand *louis d'or* to fund the enterprise. Only seven men formed the Prince's entourage on board the frigate *Du Teillay*: Francis Strickland, an English Jacobite; three Irishmen, including Colonel John O'Sullivan, who had served in the French army and who later became a close adviser to the Prince; Sir Thomas Sheridan, Charles's old tutor; Aeneas MacDonald, a relative of the MacDonalds of Kinlochmoidart involved in Parisian banking; and the Marquess of Tullibardine, who had fought in the 1715 and 1719 campaigns, but was now nearly 50 and suffering badly from gout. Together, these men have become known as the Seven Men of Moidart. The *Du Teillay*, with its small

'Bonnie Prince Charlie' after Culloden. Charming, energetic, personally brave and extremely well-mannered, the 'Young Pretender' possessed qualities which contributed both to his contemporary popularity and the many myths about him spawned after the '45. (Corbis)

knot of adventurers, sat off Belle Isle awaiting its escort, *L'Elisabeth* (64 guns), which would convey some of the arms in addition to 700 men, and ensure that the Prince reached his destination.

Once *L'Elisabeth* arrived, the expedition set out with a plan to sail around Ireland and land on the west coast of Scotland, but on the first day of the journey his plans went awry when the two ships were sighted by HMS *Lion*. In the course of the ensuing action *L'Elisabeth* fared the worst, suffering enough damage to oblige her to put back into Brest. The *Du Teillay*, which had remained aloof from the fight, survived the encounter without injury, but the absence of *L'Elisabeth* denied the expedition of half its manpower and equipment. Notwithstanding the poor prospects that this foretold, the Prince insisted that the expedition proceed. He still possessed funds, his adherents and a determination to open his campaign in Scotland with a flourish.

Despite the frantic search for the Prince by Royal Navy vessels, Charles's frigate managed to reach the Outer Hebrides, where a longboat guided his ship through inland waters to a harbour on the tiny island of Eriskay. There he landed on 23 July 1745. The rebellion had begun.

Raising the standard of revolt

Charles's arrival did make for an impressive show of force, and the following morning he discovered that the chief of the MacLeods and Alexander MacDonald of Sleat were not prepared to support him unless he could supply troops. Barring this, Charles was advised to return to France until such time as he could furnish something tangible. It appeared that he had indeed exaggerated the extent of support he could expect to receive in the Highlands, and yet he could not now withdraw, for a British warship sat outside the harbour, only barred from entering owing to adverse winds. Nevertheless, remaining in the Highlands offered a better prospect than withdrawing into likely

Erecting the standard of the Young Pretender. When Prince Charles read out his manifesto he did so in the name of his father, 'James VIII', proclaiming himself regent. (The Bridgeman Art Library)

capture; so under cover of darkness and profiting by a favourable shift in the wind, the Prince boarded the *Du Teillay* and made for the Isle of Skye, where he landed around noon on 25 July at Loch nan Uamh, near Moidart, on the west coast of the Highlands. This was the country of the MacDonalds of Clanranald. Aeneas MacDonald duly went ashore to gauge the level of support in the area. The small group of MacDonalds who returned aboard the frigate for a conference offered little more encouragement than the previous day: coming out in revolt without foreign assistance struck them as a hopeless cause, unleashing forces against which they could offer no adequate defence. Quite under what circumstances the young Prince managed to persuade the MacDonalds to reconsider is not known – some say on the basis of an emotional appeal – but they had the dubious honour of being the first clan to rally to the Prince's cause.

This initial element of support gave Charles the confidence he required to proceed further, prompting him and his party to land at Moidart with all the supplies aboard the *Du Teillay*, which the Prince ordered back to France. Buoyed by initial success, the Prince sent out an appeal, calling upon John Murray of Broughton and James Drummond, titular Duke of Perth. But everything hinged on the attitude of Donald Cameron of Lochiel, for clan chiefs already sympathetic to the Jacobite cause had pledged only to join a rebellion if Lochiel gave his blessing to the design. Lochiel, like so many Highland chiefs, openly expressed his apprehensions that without foreign aid a rebellion was doomed to failure and thus the Prince could not depend upon them. Against this reluctance, the Prince argued that no time would be more propitious, for nearly the whole of the British Army was overseas, for the most part

The Jacobite Rebellions

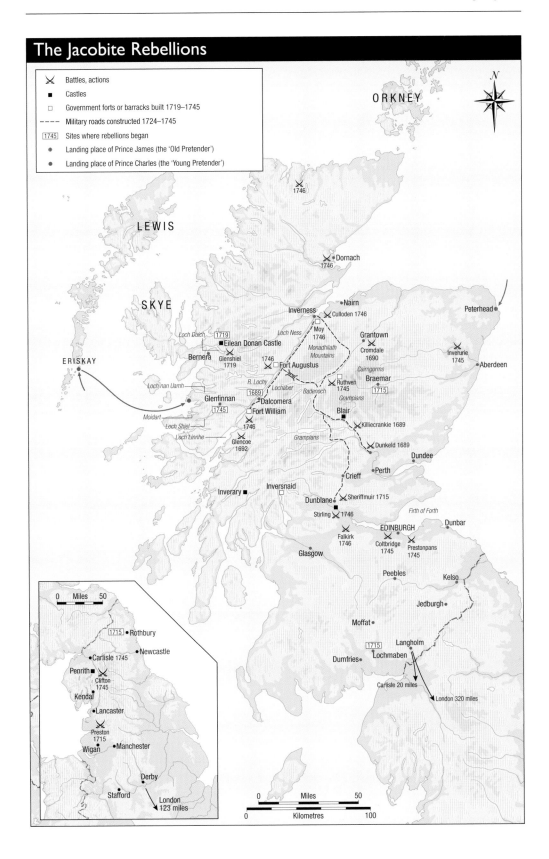

✕	Battles, actions
■	Castles
☐	Government forts or barracks built 1719–1745
----	Military roads constructed 1724–1745
1745	Sites where rebellions began
●	Landing place of Prince James (the 'Old Pretender')
●	Landing place of Prince Charles (the 'Young Pretender')

ORKNEY

LEWIS

SKYE

ERISKAY

✕ 1746

✕ Dornach
1746

Inverness
✕ Nairn
✕ Culloden 1746
Peterhead

Loch Duich
1719
■ Eilean Donan Castle
Bernera Glenshiel
1719

Moy
1746
☐ Fort Augustus
Loch Ness

Monadhliath
Mountains

Grantown
✕ Cromdale
1690

✕ Inverurie
1745
Aberdeen

Loch nan Uamh
R. Lochy
Lochaber
1689
Glenfinnan
●Dalcomera
1745
Moidart
☐ Fort William
✕
1746
Loch Shiel
Loch Linnhe
✕ Glencoe
1692

Cairngorms

✕ Ruthven
1745
Badenoch

Braemar
1715

Grampians

Blair ■
✕ Killiecrankie 1689

Grampians

✕ Dunkeld 1689
Dundee

Crieff ● Perth

Inverary ■

Inversnaid
☐

Dunblane
✕ Sheriffmuir 1715
● Stirling ✕ 1746

Firth of Forth

Falkirk
1746
✕
Glasgow
Coltbridge
1745
EDINBURGH
✕
Prestonpans
1745
Dunbar

Peebles
Kelso

Moffat

Jedburgh

1715 Langholm
Dumfries ● Lochmaben

Carlisle 20 miles
London 320 miles

Inset map

0   Miles   50

1715 ● Rothbury
● Newcastle
● Carlisle 1745
Penrith ■ ✕
Clifton
1745
Kendal
● Lancaster
✕
Preston
1715
Wigan ● Manchester

Derby

Stafford London
123 miles

0   Miles   50
0   Kilometres   100

committed to the campaign in Flanders against Marshal de Saxe, who led more numerous forces than the British. In Scotland itself the government could only depend upon a few recently raised regiments, all Scottish loyalist militia units, with no experience in the field. Once the Highlanders prevailed over such numerically inferior opponents, the Prince's father would then be able to prevail upon the French for material aid – and, above all, troops – whereupon his supporters within Britain would flock to his cause. These arguments proved persuasive and Lochiel threw in his hat, signalling a decisive moment in the rebellion, for it triggered the automatic compliance of several other clan chiefs. The Prince and his new supporters now laid plans for a rendezvous to take place at Glenfinnan, beside Loch Shiel, on 19 August, at which the MacDonalds, the Stewarts of Ardshiel, and the Camerons would gather.

But even before formal hostilities began, the Jacobite cause gained a boost when the Camerons and MacDonalds of Keppoch captured a detachment of government troops sent to reinforce the garrison of Fort William, one of a chain of three forts (the others being Fort Augustus and Fort George) extending along the Great Glen which divided the Highlands. An otherwise inconsequential action, this episode raised morale out of all expectation. Only two days later, Murray of Broughton arrived in the Prince's camp and accepted his appointment as secretary. On the 19th, between 700 and 800 Camerons arrived at Glenfinnan, though they were short of weapons, while the Marquess of Tullibardine displayed a newly made standard of white, blue and red. The Prince addressed his followers with a less than inspiring speech and shortly thereafter MacDonald of Keppoch arrived with 300 men and a handful of MacLeods. The rebellion was gathering steam.

Charles was well aware that much depended on his ability to appeal to the Scots as a Scottish prince, even if that image would require modification in the event that he chose to take the campaign into England. In the short term, therefore, he began to acquaint himself with everything Scottish, adopted Highland dress and learned a bit of Gaelic. Meanwhile, news of the Prince's arrival in Scotland had now reached England, where King George II had returned from Hanover and put a price of £30,000 on Charles's head – a vast sum at the time. If the English were resolved to the Hanoverian line, the Highland Scots were not, for most – and many in the Lowlands – despised the union with England. Irrespective of the Stuarts' right to claim the throne, the issue of the Act of Union alone constituted a vital issue around which Scots of many stripes might potentially unite.

Outmanoeuvring Cope

From the outset of the rebellion the Prince faced the fundamental problem that he could not draw upon the entire Highland population, estimated at about 30,000 clansmen of fighting age, as a military force. Only a very small proportion of these numbers actually materialized and even then, partly owing to the disarmament policies of 1715 and 1719, those clans who clung to their hopes of a Stuart restoration did not possess the resources to mount an offensive. Many, it is true, had defied the legislation requiring the surrender of their arms, but others still could not furnish the necessary quantities of weapons and equipment needed to place their forces on a proper footing. On the other hand, Charles had never assumed that he would have to oppose government forces with the Highlanders alone, and consequently had written an appeal for aid to Louis XV prior to embarking for Scotland. Thereafter, the Prince continued to reassure his followers of the likelihood of French support, and only a victory in the field, he argued, could guarantee this. It was a prospect made all the more difficult by the fact that loyalties in the Highlands were divided, not least owing to the influential Lord President of the Court of Session, Duncan Forbes of Culloden, who as a staunch opponent of Jacobitism did his utmost to discourage the clans from aiding the Prince. Forbes' role would profoundly affect the course of events. Not only did he persuade some originally inclined towards the Prince to reconsider their duty, but he was thought so influential that he could have brought most of the clans against the government, had he chosen to wield his influence in the Jacobites' favour.

By the first week of August news of the Prince's arrival had reached Edinburgh, where the garrison made vague preparations for defence, though few thought realistic the prospect of a Jacobite advance on the capital. Officials in London knew little of the nature of the revolt and of the Prince's movements, but neither they, nor their counterparts in Edinburgh, believed at this initial stage that the rebellion posed a genuinely serious threat, and thus made no substantial efforts to oppose it. Indeed, Scottish officials regarded the rebels as little more than rabble, whose defeat was only a matter of time. True, Jacobite forces remained small in number and hardly presented the picture of a highly-trained or even well-armed fighting force; but the government's assessment of the threat they posed looked increasingly

rash and the rebels took advantage of the government's relative indolence to raise men, supplies and arms.

Having said this, the government was not idle. On the same day as the clans met at Glenfinnan, Sir John Cope, commander-in-chief of the regular forces in Scotland, was in the midst of proceeding from Edinburgh to Stirling, in order to assume command of forces in the field, seek out the Prince's army and destroy it. Sir John had joined the Army as a cornet in a cavalry regiment in 1707 and subsequently assumed the colonelcy of several units in succession. An MP for three different constituencies from 1722 to 1741, he rose to became a brigadier in 1735, a major-general four years later and a lieutenant-general in 1743. When the rebellion broke out Cope was commander-in-chief in Scotland and responsibility for quelling the rising fell to him.

Passage of the Highland army beside a loch during the first weeks of the rising. Jacobite numbers swelled as they moved from Glenfinnan to meet Cope's small force, confident that foreign aid, especially from France, would eventually arrive. (Author's collection)

In the meantime, in addition to the regular regiments led by Cope, the Lord President oversaw the raising of independent companies of troops in the north, which would be placed under the command of the Earl of Loudoun. In addition to these and the existing garrison of regular troops in Scotland under Cope, the government could also deploy nine companies of troops recently raised for service with their parent units, then serving abroad. Some of these in fact had defected to the Jacobites and most were greatly below strength, but under the circumstances the government would make use of whatever resources it could gather in Scotland while the bulk of the army was committed overseas, with no prospect of immediate recall. Charles felt he had reason to be confident – a position not altogether unrealistic in light of the authorities' prevarication.

Cope reached Stirling on 19 August, the day that the Prince's standard was raised at Loch Shiel, and prepared to pursue the rebels via the Highland road which ran through Crieff and the town of Taybridge to Fort Augustus. His march, with 1,500 men, four light field guns and four mortars, began on the following day. He left a regiment of dragoons at Stirling and another at Leith, since mounted troops could not manage the rough terrain. Short of trained gunners and burdened by wagons stacked with arms intended to equip the volunteers he hoped to gather on the march, Cope found progress slow. In the fashion typical of 18th century armies, the troops were accompanied by a vast train of carts and other vehicles carrying several weeks' supplies and provisions – all perhaps necessary when campaigning in an area of limited resources – but a colossal encumbrance and hence a substantial hindrance to speed. The expected turnout of loyal Highlanders never materialized, though 40 men from Lord Loudoun's regiment joined Cope's force at Taybridge.

Both sides were now moving slowly on converging paths. The day after Cope left Stirling, Charles's army set out from Glenfinnan and proceeded towards the mountain of Corrieyairack, where he could block Cope's path to Fort Augustus. In order to speed his progress so as to arrive before Cope, the Prince ordered all superfluous baggage and equipment to be left behind, including 12 of the 20 guns conveyed from France. Ironically, thanks to one of the military roads constructed by General Wade across the Highlands 20 years before, the Jacobites reached the mountain first, whereupon they built entrenchments in order to ambush Cope's troops in the passes. The Prince's numbers had grown by this time: the Stewarts of Appin supplied 280 men, the MacDonalds of Clanranald brought with them 300, 250 Camerons had joined, and the MacDonalds of Glengarry and the Grants of Glenmoriston supplied a combined force of 400. With such numbers the rebels, although inferior in terms of equipment, training and organization, now outnumbered Cope's force. Morale was high and the Highlanders desired nothing more than an opportunity to demonstrate their martial prowess.

On 25 August, Cope received intelligence at Dalnacardoch of the Jacobites' intention to engage him under unfavourable circumstances at Corrieyairack Pass during the course of his march to Fort Augustus. He continued his advance, reaching Dalwhinnie the next day, when he received confirmation of the rebels' movements and intentions. Still 20 miles from the Jacobites' camp, Cope decided that he could not confront the enemy in prepared positions and instead ordered his army to Inverness, a course of action which avoided the humiliation of a retreat to Stirling, and kept alive the intention to ultimately bring his army into action. The Highlanders duly awaited the arrival of Cope's men, who never appeared. Marching along the Inverness road and resting for the night at Ruthven, Cope had foiled Jacobite plans to surprise him in rough ground; only when some deserters from Cope's contingent of Highlanders reached Jacobite lines did Charles become aware of his opponent's altered line of march.

Cope's failure to confront and defeat the rebels at this initial stage of the campaign –

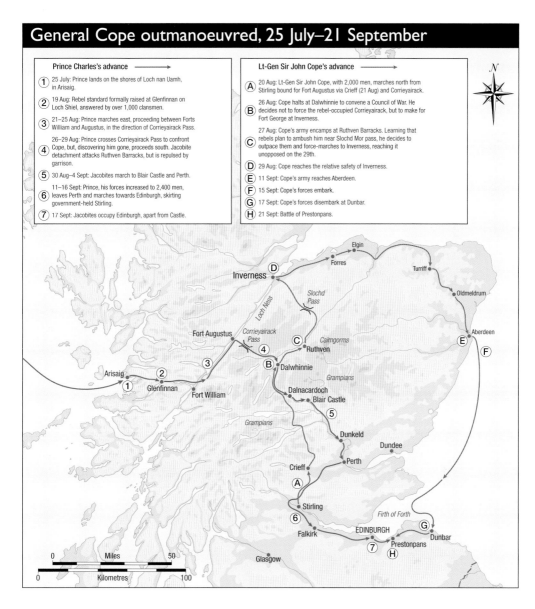

General Cope outmanoeuvred, 25 July–21 September

Prince Charles's advance →

(1) 25 July: Prince lands on the shores of Loch nan Uamh, in Arisaig.

(2) 19 Aug: Rebel standard formally raised at Glenfinnan on Loch Shiel, answered by over 1,000 clansmen.

(3) 21–25 Aug: Prince marches east, proceeding between Forts William and Augustus, in the direction of Corrieyairack Pass.

(4) 26–29 Aug: Prince crosses Corrieyairack Pass to confront Cope, but, discovering him gone, proceeds south. Jacobite detachment attacks Ruthven Barracks, but is repulsed by garrison.

(5) 30 Aug–4 Sept: Jacobites march to Blair Castle and Perth.

(6) 11–16 Sept: Prince, his forces increased to 2,400 men, leaves Perth and marches towards Edinburgh, skirting government-held Stirling.

(7) 17 Sept: Jacobites occupy Edinburgh, apart from Castle.

Lt-Gen Sir John Cope's advance →

(A) 20 Aug: Lt-Gen Sir John Cope, with 2,000 men, marches north from Stirling bound for Fort Augustus via Crieff (21 Aug) and Corrieyairack.

(B) 26 Aug: Cope halts at Dalwhinnie to convene a Council of War. He decides not to force the rebel-occupied Corrieyairack, but to make for Fort George at Inverness.

(C) 27 Aug: Cope's army encamps at Ruthven Barracks. Learning that rebels plan to ambush him near Slochd Mor pass, he decides to outpace them and force-marches to Inverness, reaching it unopposed on the 29th.

(D) 29 Aug: Cope reaches the relative safety of Inverness.

(E) 11 Sept: Cope's army reaches Aberdeen.

(F) 15 Sept: Cope's forces embark.

(G) 17 Sept: Cope's forces disembark at Dunbar.

(H) 21 Sept: Battle of Prestonpans.

and particularly his decision to divert his course for Inverness – had far-reaching implications, for it exposed Edinburgh and the Lowlands to Jacobite occupation if Charles decided to proceed south. He did. Rather than seeking battle with Cope in the north, as originally planned, the rebels could not resist the chance to take the lightly defended Scottish capital. In the meantime, Cope's army, its rations almost exhausted, struggled through the Grampians with much distance yet to be covered, not reaching Inverness until 29 August. In the event, the

Highlands had proved the most formidable of regions – much more challenging than Cope had imagined. In having outmanoeuvred government forces and drawn them into a forbidding region, Charles had achieved an initial psychological advantage with, as yet, barely a shot having been fired.

At Inverness, Cope met with Duncan Forbes, the latter then seeking to attract recruits from clans perceived to be, or openly declaring themselves to be, loyal to the government. At the same time, Cope took steps to strengthen the Lowlands by

Colonel James Gardiner, who led a regiment of government dragoons. While the Jacobite army moved south against Edinburgh, Gardiner's unit was supposed to be guarding the river Forth at Stirling, but withdrew on the rebels' approach. At Prestonpans Highlanders actually charged Gardiner's dragoons, slashing at the horses' muzzles and driving them from the field, leaving Cope's infantry unsupported. Gardiner himself refused to join in the rout and was killed. (Author's collection)

organizing transports to Aberdeen to convey his troops south by sea in time to march on Leith, from there intercepting the rebels before they could reach Edinburgh. Time was of the essence: on 4 September he led his troops out of Inverness on the road to Aberdeen, from where they embarked on the 16th, having absorbed only 200 loyal Highlanders under George Munro of Culcairn – nothing like the result Cope had expected in response to his recruitment drive.

The Prince had long since shelved plans to pursue Cope and had instead led his army through the mountains of Blair Atholl and into the Lowlands, welcoming into its ranks men furnished by Macpherson of Cluny. The advance guard of the rebels entered Perth on 3 September and the following day the Prince

rode in wearing Highland costume – a deliberate ploy to encourage local support, though it is vital to emphasize that he still intended to unite the whole of Britain behind the Stuart claim. For the moment, however, such a lofty aim demanded execution in stages; thus far he commanded little more than 1,800 men, with supporters soon augmenting this when James Drummond, the Duke of Perth, together with Lord George Murray, brought in contingents. These men were to hold joint command of Jacobite forces, a situation fraught with so many difficulties that at one phase, by a bizarre and unworkable expedient, they led the army on alternate days to avoid falling into disputes over seniority.

But such friction lay in the future; for the moment, the occupation of Perth, in conjunction with Cope's retreat, did much to encourage rebel morale. With the city now in their hands, the Jacobites began to levy contributions from the local populace and attract donations from well-disposed wealthy families. Outlying regions also fell subject to taxation and by the time Charles's army left the city on 11 September he had not only raised substantial and much-needed funds, but also augmented the strength of his forces to approximately 2,400 men – thanks not only to the contingents brought by Murray and the Duke of Perth, but additional men from the clans MacGregor and Robertson.

On 13 September the Jacobite army crossed the Forth about eight miles from Stirling, by which time the authorities in Edinburgh had begun to appreciate the seriousness of the situation. Horrified at the prospect of occupation, they could do nothing in the short term to fortify the city, whose walls mounted no artillery and, in any event, offered no real protection to an attacker, for in places they stood no more than a few feet tall. Only the castle, a formidable structure with a garrison of 600 troops and a small complement of guns, could offer any reliable form of resistance; but even then its commander, the 87-year-old gout-ridden General Guest, relied on his men to carry him around on a stretcher. Still, the city's authorities had begun to raise volunteers on 9 September for purposes of augmenting the strength of the City Guard, but nothing in the way of an adequate garrison stood to oppose the approaching enemy. Meanwhile, Cope made strenuous efforts to reach the city before the Prince. The vagaries of the wind, however, prevented him from landing any closer to Edinburgh than Dunbar, where he disembarked his troops on 17 September, with the guns following the day after.

At the same time, in his attempts to reach the same objective as Sir John, Charles had met no opposition in crossing the Fords of Frew and he occupied Linlithgow on the 15th. By the afternoon of the following day he had reached the outskirts of the capital and sent a summons to the Provost and Magistrates, calling on them to surrender without a fight in exchange for a guarantee that his troops would not harm the city's inhabitants and their property. Ominously, the conditions contained indistinct threats in the event of refusal. Even before this, the city authorities had already botched plans for the capital's defence; more than once, troops had marched in and out of the city in an ineffectual display of force, before returning within the walls with nothing to show for their pointless bravado. Worse still, by the time the Prince had sent his summons, no word of Cope's approach had arrived, leaving the city's councillors without a hand to play.

The authorities duly sent a deputation to Charles's headquarters to negotiate terms, but in the meantime word came of Cope's disembarkation, prompting officials to reconsider their position in light of improving prospects. Emboldened by new circumstances, the city council delayed proceedings by altering its proposals and placing the volunteers back on the alert. The Jacobites, brooking no delay, received with suspicion a new set of deputies dispatched to the Prince's camp in a transparent ruse to prolong discussions. After the failure of talks in the early hours of the 17th, the city's negotiators were returned

by coach. When the Nether Bow port was opened to allow the coach to pass back out of the city and return to the Jacobite lines, several hundred Highlanders, hidden in darkness, forced their way in, disarmed the sentries at the other gates and overpowered the town guard. By dawn the city lay in rebel hands – just as Cope was disembarking his army at Dunbar.

The whole of the Jacobite army entered the city on the 17th – a remarkable achievement and without so much as a major military encounter to facilitate it. The Castle, on the other hand, remained defiant, and the best Charles's troops could do was to blockade it for the whole term of occupation to prevent the garrison from sallying out and relieving the city. In the meantime, while the authorities remained sullen and embittered, the inhabitants looked on the invaders in bemused fashion, regarding the affair as something of a giant carnival, for the Highlanders with their peculiar array of weapons and often unshod feet made for remarkable viewing, as of course did the Prince and the Highland chiefs who attracted enormous attention in the streets. But celebrate as they might, the Jacobites had yet to be tested in battle; the taking of Edinburgh offered no evidence as to their true mettle and only the inability of the city officials to organize some sort of hasty defence prevented them from becoming stalled, just on the point when Cope might have arrived to preserve the capital in government hands.

While the rebel army established its camp just outside the city at Duddingston, Cope marched out of Dunbar on the 19th and advanced on Edinburgh, bent on engaging the Prince's forces and liberating the city. That evening government troops encamped at Haddington, while in a meeting that night the Prince and his military commanders decided that their rebel army must decamp in the morning and confront Cope before he reached the capital. The Prince's army, almost entirely infantry, had meanwhile risen slightly in strength to about 2,400 men; not, as hoped, from men locally recruited in

Prince Charles enters Edinburgh. One resident described the polyglot rebel forces thus: 'I observed there armes, they were guns of different syses, and some of innormowos [enormous] length, some with butts turned up lick a heren, some tyed with puck threed to the stock, some without locks and some matchlocks, some had swords over ther showlder instead of guns, one or two had pitchforks, and some bits of sythes upon poles with a cleek [a hook], some [had] old Lochaber axes.' (Mary Evans Picture Library)

Edinburgh, where the populace tolerated rather than actively supported the Young Pretender, but from several hundred men drawn from the clan Maclachlan, together with small numbers of men from Atholl. At the same time several men of prominence joined the Jacobites, including Lord Elcho, Lord Balmerino and the Earl of Kellie. On the other hand, little in the way of additional arms were to be found at Edinburgh, for the inhabitants had sensibly sequestered their weapons in the Castle, though some captured muskets served partially to arm those Highlanders as yet without firearms. Thus variously armed, the Jacobite army left its camp at Duddingston on 20 September and proceeded to Preston, based on intelligence that Cope's army was advancing to there. Cope, at the same time, making for the flat ground between the

villages of Seaton and Preston, had sent Lord Loudoun to scout the area, upon which he returned and reported that the Jacobites were approaching.

Prestonpans, 21 September 1745

Cope reached the conclusion that he could safely establish his position on open ground a short distance north of Tranent. He initially faced west, with the village of Prestonpans to his front, in the expectation that this would be the direction from which the rebels would attack. It proved an excellent defensive position, offering protection on three sides: Tranent, with various coal pits, hedges, ditches and a large, seemingly unfordable swamp to the south, on the enemy's left. To the west lay the sea and the villages of Prestonpans and Preston, in the latter of which stood Colonel Gardiner's house with its high walls and Preston House park, surrounded by a 10ft wall of its own. To the north lay the sea and the village of Cockenzie. Lord George Murray, the Jacobite commander, made the mistake of attempting to occupy the high ground, which commanded a view of the government position from the south, without consulting those knowledgeable of the ground. When his forces reached the top of the hill they found that the terrain would not suit an attack, for at the base of the hill lay the marsh on which was anchored Cope's left, known as Tranent Meadows.

When he found the rebels now confronting him from the south instead of from the west, Cope redeployed to face south, thus holding a better position than before, with the marsh immediately to his front. Having decided that an attack from the south was ill-advised, the rebels decided to traverse the swamp and attack Cope from the east on flat, open ground. They marched in the early hours of the 21st using a narrow footpath identified by a local man. The movement was perceived by barking dogs in Tranent

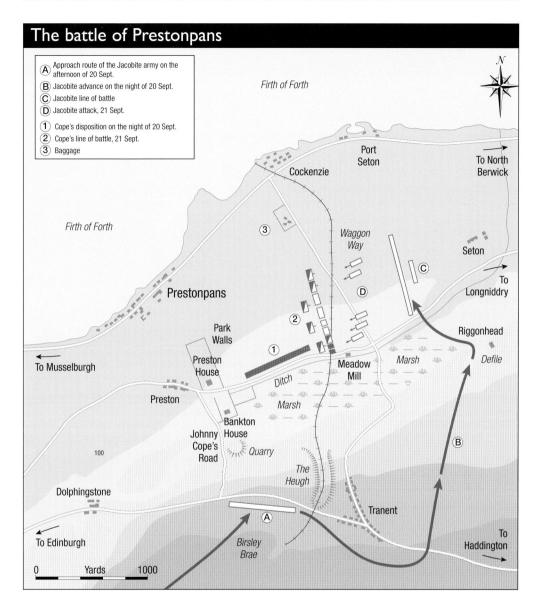

The battle of Prestonpans

(A) Approach route of the Jacobite army on the afternoon of 20 Sept.
(B) Jacobite advance on the night of 20 Sept.
(C) Jacobite line of battle
(D) Jacobite attack, 21 Sept.

(1) Cope's disposition on the night of 20 Sept.
(2) Cope's line of battle, 21 Sept.
(3) Baggage

Firth of Forth

Port Seton

To North Berwick

Cockenzie

Firth of Forth

(3)

Waggon Way

Seton

(C)

To Longniddry

Prestonpans

(D)

Riggonhead

Park Walls

(2)

Defile

To Musselburgh

Preston House

(1)

Meadow Mill

Marsh

Ditch

Marsh

Preston

Bankton House

Johnny Cope's Road

Quarry

The Heugh

(B)

100

Dolphingstone

Tranent

To Edinburgh

(A)

Birsley Brae

To Haddington

0   Yards   1000

and observed by a mounted government picket at Riggonhead. Cope accordingly shifted his army again, to face east, with the marsh to his right. He ordered back the pickets to the main body, formed his lines and rode across the front to encourage his men, who in all numbered about 2,100.

The 44th Foot occupied the right, the 46th the left, and eight companies of the 47th and two from the 6th stood in the centre. All his artillery – four mortars and six 1½-pounders – were positioned on the right, but this small complement was rendered

useless by the desertion of its civilian drivers and the naval gunners sent by HMS *Fox*. Only two officers and four men were available to man ten pieces.

Cope had a total of 650 dragoons. On the right stood squadrons of the 13th, and on the left two squadrons of the 14th. One squadron from each regiment was held in reserve. The rebels had only 36 cavalry and about 2,300 infantry, divided into two parts, plus a reserve. The considerable gap between the two bodies of the rebel army gave Cope, viewing them through the mist, the mistaken impression that the forces opposite were greater than they were, and that his left might be threatened. He consequently ordered two guns to be shifted from the right to the left, but the civilian drivers and gunners had since abandoned their posts.

With 950 men of the left wing Murray launched an attack through the mist across a newly harvested cornfield. These charged obliquely towards the government right across the 200 yards that separated the rival forces. As they advanced the sun broke through and the two sides could see one another clearly. Some accounts claim the handful of men attached to the artillery fired their pieces and ran; others that the guns had already been abandoned and that Colonel Whitefoord and another officer fired five of the guns and all the mortars. Whatever the truth, the effect on the charging Highlanders was momentary and ineffective. Moreover, Cope's right was crowded by the return of the outposts, such that the 13th Dragoons had little space for manoeuvre. The front squadron under Colonel Whitney, as well as that under Colonel Gardiner – placed behind for want of space – refused to charge, and after a single volley from the rebels the horsemen fled.

On the left was equal disaster. As the Highlanders charged, the 14th Dragoons were given no order to attack and when their commander was shot the men fled, taking the reserve with them. Having fired their customary volley, the Highlanders cast aside their muskets and closed in with their broadswords. The infantry found their right flank as well as their front under attack and broke up in a matter of minutes. A detachment of 20 men of the 44th stood its ground in a ditch until surrounded and forced to surrender. All the infantry rapidly melted away and although 450 of the cavalry were rallied by Cope, Lord Loudoun, Home and others, these resolutely refused to engage the enemy. Nor would the fleeing infantry stand, despite threats made by officers wielding pistols. Total rout ensued and soon the handful of officers and infantry who still held their ground were obliged to

join the fugitives. The chaos enabled the clansmen to inflict severe losses on Cope, who retreated first to Coldstream and on to Berwick the following day.

Thus, in an action lasting less than ten minutes, Cope's army was put to flight and lost more than half its effective strength in prisoners. The rebels lost about 35 killed and 75 wounded. The government side suffered about 150 killed and at least 1,000 made prisoner, plus all their baggage. Cope's military chest, containing between £3,000 and £4,000, also fell into the Prince's hands.

Prestonpans was a great though temporary blow to the Hanoverian cause and conversely raised the morale of the Jacobites, who could no longer be held in contempt by their enemies as a mob of savages. 'The greatest advantage we derived from it,' Chevalier de Johnstone, Lord George Murray's aide-de-camp, wrote, 'was the reputation that the Prince's army acquired in the onset; which determined many of his partisans who were yet wavering to declare themselves openly in his favour.' Of at least equal significance, the outcome of the battle left Scotland almost entirely bereft of government troops, with the exception of Edinburgh Castle, Stirling and the Highland forts. The Jacobites, it seemed, were now a serious force to be reckoned with.

The march south

If the Jacobites needed a triumph to encourage faith in their ability to take on and defeat regular forces, it also left them with the impression of invincibility. So emboldened, the Prince wished to pursue Cope to Berwick. This proved impossible, however, owing to desertions sizeable enough as to render another pitched battle inadvisable, at least in the short term. The army, so recently blooded, could not afford a setback at this point lest it lose momentum and spoil the euphoric atmosphere following Prestonpans. Any evacuation of Edinburgh, moreover, threatened to jeopardize the benefits to be derived from using the capital as a base for recruitment, for Jacobite leaders now reckoned that, impressed by the tangible display of the Highlanders' fighting ability, volunteers would begin to flock to the cause in large numbers.

Politically, Charles faced a difficult choice. While abolishing the Act of Union would be a popular decision, and a higher aspiration for most Highlanders than the re-establishment of the Stuarts on the throne, the Prince always viewed his mission as recovering the entire kingdom, including Ireland, and by abolishing the Union he would rapidly alienate English public opinion. To appear merely to be championing a narrow Scottish cause was to threaten the whole movement. To lend credibility to his cause, he therefore deemed it vital to take the rebellion south to London, gathering Jacobite adherents in England as he went. Still, it was all very well issuing a public statement to the effect that he intended to re-establish freedom of religion and act to protect the laws and liberties of a free people; since such rights already existed as far as most of those loyal to the Hanoverian line were concerned, promises for their return struck them as empty and did nothing to allay their suspicions of a Catholic prince, still associated with the absolutism they had cast off during the Glorious Revolution more than half a century before.

Charles's council strongly recommended maintaining the army in Scotland; consequently, his forces continued their occupation of Edinburgh for almost six weeks after Prestonpans. Charles busied himself trying to woo as yet uncommitted clans and persuading Louis XV to provide more than merely moral support for his cause, while Forbes waged his own propaganda campaign in Scotland against the Jacobites. The inhabitants of Edinburgh itself showed little inclination to join the Prince, but Charles enjoyed rather better success in outlying regions, drawing on the support of John Gordon of Glenbucket of Aberdeenshire, with 400 men; Lord Pitsligo with a corps of well-armed and

well-mounted troops from the counties of Aberdeen and Banff; Mackinnon of Mackinnon with 120 men from Skye; and Lord Ogilvy with several hundred followers from Angus.

Meanwhile, if the French refused to send troops, they appreciated that the rebellion could not survive without arms. In October, three ships arrived at Montrose and Stonehaven with weapons and equipment and a small party of French artillerymen, in addition to a representative from the court of Louis XV. The rebels expected rather more, but the Prince placated his followers with assurances that it merely represented the first of several shipments, with foreign troops to come too. In the meantime, they could not remain static forever, for even while they attracted supporters from their base in Edinburgh, the British government was fully occupied in gathering troops in England for a renewed offensive. Troops recalled from Flanders, together with Dutch forces, now stood on English soil, and by the end of October the Prince learned that a force under Field Marshal Wade had reached Newcastle. On the 19th, the Duke of Cumberland, third son of George II, was recalled from Holland, and shortly thereafter several regiments of foot and horse arrived home. In addition to the forces dispatched to the north-east, major bodies stood in the Midlands and along the coast of south-east England. Supplementing all these, volunteer units, albeit often only of company strength, were assembling the length and breadth of the country. Meanwhile, the king appointed the Duke of Cumberland commander-in-chief of forces at home; he established his headquarters with the force in the Midlands.

While Charles continued to argue for a strike into England so as to confront Wade's army before it became too powerful to overcome, Lord George Murray advocated waiting until the army had benefited from growing numbers and further training. If rebel forces were to cross the border, he argued, they should proceed through the

county of Cumberland, allowing them draw
upon Jacobite supporters from the north,
particularly areas believed to be broadly
sympathetic such as Northumberland and
possibly Lancashire. Carlisle appeared the
best place for the army to establish itself,
with any further volunteers from Scotland
still within reach. The army duly left
Edinburgh in two columns, one under
Prince Charles Edward and Lord George
Murray, and another under the Marquess
of Tullibardine and the Duke of Perth, who
would take a different route to Carlisle. The
army now stood at what on the Continent
only qualified as division strength:
5,000 infantry and 500 cavalry, plus enough
provisions to maintain this force for the
coming campaign. However the men, rested
from several weeks' stay in Edinburgh,
boasted proper arms and clothing and no
longer hailed entirely from the Highlands,
for in addition to 13 clan regiments were
five from the Lowlands, plus 13 pieces of
artillery, of which six came from France and
the remainder from the field at Prestonpans.

The Jacobite army marched out of
Edinburgh on 1 November, much to the relief
of the population, but for many Highlanders
the notion of fighting at such a considerable
distance from home did not prove popular,
with increasing numbers of desertions the
result. On reaching Kelso, Charles's column
halted for the day before proceeding to
Jedburgh. On 9 November it reached the
outskirts of Carlisle, meeting there the force
under Tullibardine, who had taken a route
through Peebles and Moffat. The garrison
of local militia under Colonel Durand held
the castle, whose guns drove off the rebels.
But they were not to be dismayed for long;
the following day the Jacobites sent word that
the town was immediately to open its gates or
face unspecified consequences. The mayor,
Thomas Patterson, wildly overestimated the
size of the force arrayed against him, and
feared the worst when news arrived that Wade
could offer no immediate relief. The public
began to panic, and although the garrison
pledged to defend the town, on 14 November
Patterson dispatched a deputation to the

Jacobite camp, which was by then established
at Brampton in order best to resist Wade if
he chose to advance. Learning from the
experience at Edinburgh, where the garrison in
the Castle had harassed the army throughout
their occupation, the Jacobites insisted on
the capitulation of both town and castle.
The Westmoreland and Cumberland militia,
appreciating that the rebels intended to assault
the town if their terms were refused, began
to lose the will to fight, and many began to
desert. The Duke of Perth accepted the town's
surrender at 10am on the 15th and the
following morning the castle followed. This
proved significant, for the fortress contained
several guns, a sizeable supply of ammunition,
100 barrels of gunpowder, and 1,000 muskets
in addition to those given up by the militia.

Ironically, the cache of arms also contained a large number of broadswords taken from the rebels at Preston in 1715.

Thus far the Jacobites had managed to confuse Wade, who remained at Newcastle. The two-pronged advance into England had fixed the field marshal in place, who occupied himself in fortifying a city which was never a rebel target. Before Wade understood that he had been duped, the Jacobites had reached Carlisle, which prompted him to break camp on 16 November and march for Hexham. Discovering the roads incapable of sustaining the movement of his army and its vast baggage train, and appreciating that Carlisle could not be retaken with the forces at his disposal, Wade returned to Newcastle.

The battle of Prestonpans, 21 September 1745. General Cope, with 2,100 troops, deployed near the coast at the village of Prestonpans, his troops facing south and his front protected by marshy ground. The Jacobites, 2,300 strong and formed on high ground to the south, crossed the morass under cover of darkness and attacked from the east, routing their inexperienced opponents in only ten minutes. (National Army Museum)

Charles, anxious to press further into England, persuaded the Council of War to proceed into Lancashire, even as reinforcements for Wade's forces were on their way north and other regulars and militia had strengthened their presence at Stirling. A Jacobite thrust further south had increasingly little to recommend it, for government troops now stood concentrated in three locations, all within reasonable

Apart from his command in the 1715–16 campaign, Field Marshal George Wade is best associated with the 250 miles of military roads which he built across the Highlands. Ironically, only the Jacobites themselves used these thoroughfares, painstakingly constructed through exceedingly rough country, during the 1745–46 campaign. (Hulton Archive/Getty)

striking distance of the rebel army, and thus far the hope of raising the English Jacobites had come to naught.

Nonetheless, the Prince's view prevailed against the opinion of most of his commanders, whom he persuaded that Jacobites in Lancashire were certain to offer themselves in service. After leaving behind a token garrison of a few hundred men, the rebels left Carlisle on 20 November, judging that it was only a matter of time before government forces converged on the town and trapped the Jacobites in place. For the Prince, striking at the enemy took on a new priority for they had to be prevented from uniting; already, each of the government armies outnumbered the total rebel forces by a factor of two to one. Any further

concentration would render them unbeatable. Moreover, the Prince claimed to have correspondence from sympathizers further south who promised that armed volunteers would appear at Preston. Such assurances continued to lend credibility to his arguments and reassured him that in due course the whole of England would rally to his standard.

Nothing of the sort occurred. The people of the villages through which the Jacobite army passed watched with a mixture of curiosity and mild anxiety at the peculiar sight of the Highlanders in their striking national dress – but the Stuart cause meant little or nothing to them. Even members of the aristocracy who privately held Jacobite sympathies took no action, for without evidence of a popular rising or military success, they could not afford to risk their lives and estates for what might amount to a disastrous enterprise.

The army camped at Preston on 27 November, with no rapturous reception or evidence of a spontaneous turnout of volunteers, armed or otherwise. Moreover, the place reminded the invaders of their defeat there in 1715, the temperature had dropped precipitately during the march, and the men required rest after their exhausting advance. At the same time, the Duke of Cumberland assumed command at Lichfield. Not a single volunteer came forward at Preston and only 180 recruits offered themselves in Manchester on the 29th. It was now plain to see that no substantial support could be expected from the English Jacobites, who in the course of the advance through the north of England never contributed more than 300 men to the Prince's army. The rebel army had hardly established itself comfortably in Manchester before it was on the move again on 1 December, based on intelligence that Cumberland's army was advancing. The Jacobites chose Derby as their next objective, deploying a ruse to convince Cumberland that the whole rebel force intended to confront him. Lord George Murray marched a small force to Congleton by way of a diversion, hoping that the Duke would amass his troops against it and thus enable the Prince's principal force to march via another route and occupy Derby. The small detachment under Lord George learned that Cumberland's force stood at approximately 2,200 cavalry and 8,000 infantry, situated about seven miles north of Stafford, where the Duke suspected – as a consequence of Lord George's presence in the area – that the rebels intended to make a westward thrust for Wales. Cumberland took the bait, while Lord George Murray's more mobile detachment easily broke contact and rejoined the Jacobite main body at Derby.

Most Jacobite officers determined that the army could not remain there for long. Wade was fast approaching and it was only a matter of time before Cumberland realized his error and reversed his direction of march; moreover, a third force, to the south, boasted a strength equal to the other two armies combined. The English Jacobites had not appeared in appreciable numbers, the French had utterly let down the cause, and even the north of England, thought to be a stronghold of Jacobite sentiment, appeared cold at best, hostile at worst. Winter conditions began to bite and though London stood only four days' march away, nothing could be expected but armed resistance from volunteers, rising daily in number, poised to challenge a Jacobite invasion force. Good fortune appeared to have accompanied the Prince this far; any further advance looked like tempting fate.

Retreat to Scotland

In the Council of War convened at Derby to consider the question, Charles expressed his determination to push on. However, the serious discontent which traced its origins at least back to Carlisle, and which at Manchester persuaded many officers that retreat offered the best hope of survival, finally bubbled to the surface, with only the Duke of Perth sharing the Prince's opinion on the proper course to pursue. The argument for retreat carried further weight when news arrived that Lord John Drummond, the Duke's brother, had reached Scotland from France with a regiment of émigré Scots as well as Irish troops in French service. These troops, in addition to men recruited to the body that remained in Scotland under Lord Strathallan, could serve to supplement the Prince's army – but only if it returned north.

Just after dawn on 6 December the Jacobite army consequently began its retreat, much to the relief of the people of Derby, on whom the troops had been billeted and many of whose possessions had disappeared. The fact that the rebels left behind large quantities of equipment suggested disorganization and flagging discipline – not an auspicious sign. Worse still, the officers did not initially reveal to the men their destination, leaving many with the impression that they were in fact seeking out Cumberland's main force. As the sky lightened the men soon began to recognize the ground over which they had trod before

Major troop movements during the rebellion

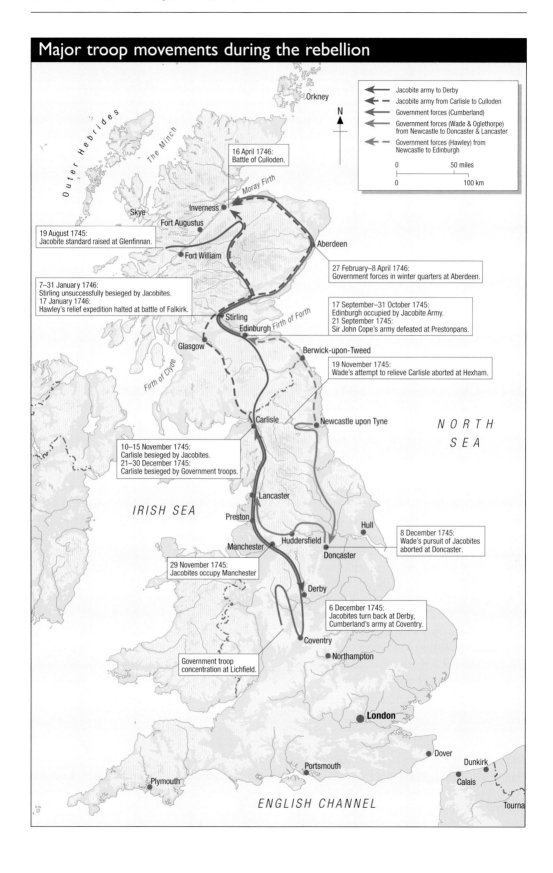

Jacobite army to Derby
Jacobite army from Carlisle to Culloden
Government forces (Cumberland)
Government forces (Wade & Oglethorpe) from Newcastle to Doncaster & Lancaster
Government forces (Hawley) from Newcastle to Edinburgh

0   50 miles
0   100 km

Orkney

Outer Hebrides

The Minch

16 April 1746:
Battle of Culloden.

Moray Firth

Inverness

Skye

Fort Augustus

19 August 1745:
Jacobite standard raised at Glenfinnan.

Fort William

Aberdeen

27 February–8 April 1746:
Government forces in winter quarters at Aberdeen.

7–31 January 1746:
Stirling unsuccessfully besieged by Jacobites.
17 January 1746:
Hawley's relief expedition halted at battle of Falkirk.

17 September–31 October 1745:
Edinburgh occupied by Jacobite Army.
21 September 1745:
Sir John Cope's army defeated at Prestonpans.

Stirling

Firth of Forth

Edinburgh

Glasgow

Firth of Clyde

Berwick-upon-Tweed

19 November 1745:
Wade's attempt to relieve Carlisle aborted at Hexham.

Carlisle

Newcastle upon Tyne

NORTH SEA

10–15 November 1745:
Carlisle besieged by Jacobites.
21–30 December 1745:
Carlisle besieged by Government troops.

IRISH SEA

Lancaster

Preston

Manchester

Huddersfield

Hull

8 December 1745:
Wade's pursuit of Jacobites aborted at Doncaster.

Doncaster

29 November 1745:
Jacobites occupy Manchester

Derby

6 December 1745:
Jacobites turn back at Derby, Cumberland's army at Coventry.

Government troop concentration at Lichfield.

Coventry

Northampton

London

Dover

Dunkirk

Portsmouth

Calais

Plymouth

ENGLISH CHANNEL

Tourna

and realized, much to their disgust, that they would never reach London. The Prince grew visibly withdrawn and depressed, for the retrograde movement signalled the shattering of a dream, and his disconsolate mood began to pervade the rank and file, whose increasing indiscipline manifested itself in the form of looting. The attitude of the public as the army returned through its previous ports of call demonstrated the turn in Jacobite fortunes. If before local people had at least feigned happiness at the arrival of the Prince and his band of misfits, now they showed open hostility. Encouraged by agents sent ahead by the government and sometimes working in tandem with local militia, civilians actively disrupted the rebels' progress by refusing to sell goods and destroying roads and bridges. A mob met the Prince's army at Manchester and although the former could not hope to oppose them with anything much more threatening than abuse and the odd projectile, the Jacobites' reception confirmed the sceptics' suspicion – if by now any confirmation were still required – that little tangible support was to be had much beyond the Highlands.

Cumberland now smelled blood. Aware that the rebels were withdrawing north, he worked assiduously to engage them as soon as possible. Wade received orders to move rapidly to intercept them. On 10 December he reached Wakefield, too late to overtake the Jacobites, who had at the same time entered Wigan. Wade then withdrew to Newcastle, leaving Cumberland, reinforced with cavalry from Wade's command, to pursue from Preston. The Jacobites continued to receive a hostile reception in the course of their retreat, not least in the refusal of villagers and townspeople to supply food, which in turn led to increased instances of looting and acts of violence. By 15 December the rebels had arrived at Kendal, where the inhabitants fired upon them. At the same time, Charles received intelligence that Wade would not leave Newcastle, suggesting that Jacobite forces could reach Scotland without interception,

but he was unaware that Cumberland, with 4,000 men, lay within two days' march. Damaged bridges and roads impeded the movement of the pursuer as much as the pursued, but with better transport and food the government forces advanced more rapidly and gradually narrowed the distance – so much so that on 18 December elements of Cumberland's force made contact with the rebel rearguard.

On 17 December the Jacobite main body arrived safely at Penrith – albeit to a populace already less keen to receive it than when it had originally passed through – but its rearguard lagged behind by about ten miles. While the sound of trumpets suggested a large body of enemy cavalry in the vicinity,

Highlanders sitting around the fire. Their appearance attracted much comment, especially in the north of England, where one hostile newspaper in Derby described them thus: 'They appear'd in general to answer the description we have all along had of them, viz. most of their main body a parcel of shabby, lousy, pitiful-look'd fellows, mix'd up with old men and boys, dress'd in dirty plaids, and as dirty shirts, without breeches, and wore their stockings made of plaid, not much above half way up their legs, and some without shoes, or next to none, and numbers of them so fatigu'd with their long march, that they really commanded our pity more than fear.' (The Stapleton Collection/The Bridgeman Art Library)

in fact the threat arose from a small force of lightly armed mounted men who fled in confusion as soon as Jacobite cavalry scurried up the slope on which they stood. The rebels thereupon resumed their advance, but after two miles government forces attacked the clansmen in the rear of the column. However, Cumberland's cavalry could not be deployed as intended as the narrow road was lined with hedges and ditches, which enabled the Jacobites to fend off repeated attacks and each time rejoin their comrades. When they reached the village of Clifton, two miles south of Penrith, elements of the Jacobite main body faced round and marched to assist their countrymen – the MacDonalds – in an effort to detach the pursuers from the rebel rear. While Charles ordered Lord George Murray not to engage his pursuers, the proximity of government forces rendered this impossible. Some government dragoons dismounted and established themselves behind a series of hedges and ditches, only to be driven off by a single Highland charge; although this skirmish took place without the Prince's blessing, he could not but be satisfied with its result.

Although a minor action, Clifton enabled the Jacobites to separate themselves temporarily from their pursuers, and by marching through the night they reached Carlisle, where the whole force including the rearguard assembled on the 19th. Reinforcements from Lord Drummond's command were expected from the north, as well as the new recruits at Perth under Lord Strathallan, but with no sign of them in the vicinity the sensible course remained a continued retreat to Scotland. The Young Pretender demonstrated his particular dislike of abandoning England by leaving a garrison of 300 to 400 men behind at Carlisle. The Prince's officers appreciated the futility of effectively abandoning these men to their fate but, as in so many matters, they bent to the will of their titular sovereign. Charles knew Cumberland possessed no heavy artillery with which to lay siege to Carlisle, but the fact remained that this could be acquired in time, and once the big guns were

committed against the city's totally inadequate defences the garrison would fall easily into enemy hands. Still, some of his troops, notwithstanding their uncertain future in England, actively sought to remain behind on account of their nationality, while the Prince appears also to have left a number of officers bearing commissions in the French Army so that, in the event of their capture, they would be accorded the status of prisoners of war rather than of rebels. Whatever the motives, at the very least the garrison could slow the advance of government forces, and on 20 December the Jacobite army left Carlisle, reaching the river Esk in the early afternoon.

Nearly unfordable due to heavy rains, the river crossing saw men wading up to their necks in places along a chain of their comrades, linked by outstretched arms to form a human bridge. After two hours the army was across, miraculously without a single loss apart from some camp followers. Once again the rebels stood on Scottish soil, having last seen it on 8 November – but now with considerably poorer prospects before them. Still, the retreat had remained orderly, for the most part, and cost little in terms of lives or deserters. As before, the Jacobites split their forces in order to confuse those in pursuit. A contingent camped in Annan in Dumfriesshire on the night of 20 December while the second bivouacked in Ecclefechan. On Christmas Day the advance guard reached Glasgow, with the main body joining up the following day. The entire campaign had covered almost 600 miles in just under two months – a remarkable effort considering the poor state of the roads and sub-zero temperatures.

True to Lord George Murray's suspicions, Cumberland acquired the heavy guns he needed to reduce the walls of Carlisle, whose garrison surrendered on 30 December – two days after the besiegers emplaced the guns and threatened the castle with bombardment. The Duke then returned to London, ordering Lieutenant-General Henry Hawley, a veteran of the 1715 campaign as well as of Dettingen and Fontenoy, to pursue

the rebels into Scotland with part of the
Duke's force. The fall of Carlisle represented
another poor decision on the part of the
Prince, who failed to heed his subordinates'
advice to withdraw all his forces from
England. Still, opportunities yet remained to
bring government troops to action in a
pitched battle on Scottish soil. Ragged and
exhausted though the Jacobites certainly
were at this point, they by no means
represented a spent force.

Events in Scotland during Charles's
absence only highlighted the fact. After some
deliberation, the clan Fraser joined the
Jacobite cause and undertook the blockade of
Fort Augustus. Lord Lewis Gordon, operating
from headquarters in Aberdeen, raised funds
and recruits from both the city itself and
bordering counties, and defeated a force of
loyal MacLeods. This was a small affair in
military terms, but one that underlined the
fact that the rebellion was never strictly a
Scots–English contest. Similarly, while the
Prince campaigned in England, Forbes,
headquartered in Inverness, continued his
efforts to mobilize support for the
government, and in so doing preserved the
extreme north for King George. On the other
hand, Jacobite volunteers converged on
Perth, where as many as 4,000 recruits added
their weight to the Young Pretender's cause.

As the government expected the rebels to
return to Edinburgh once news arrived of
their departure from England, troops duly
left Stirling to defend the capital. The Prince
was unlikely to remain long in Glasgow, for
its residents were known for their
Hanoverian sympathies and attachment to
the Protestant Succession. More than 100 of
his men deserted in the city, where ten times
this number had already come out for King
George. Finding itself amongst a hostile
population, the rebels left Glasgow on 3
January 1746 and proceeded towards Stirling
with a view to taking both the city and the
castle. As on at least two previous occasions,
the Jacobites divided their forces, with the
Prince leading one column to Bannockburn
via Kilsyth, with orders for Lord John
Drummond to link up with him, and the

Stirling. The Jacobites besieged the city and castle with
9,000 men from 1–16 January 1746, but when Murray
marched to oppose Hawley's relief column of 7,000
troops, rebel numbers around the city fell to only 1,000.
After Hawley's defeat at Falkirk, the Jacobites returned in
earnest to besiege Stirling Castle. (Author's collection)

second column under Lord George Murray
advancing on Falkirk via Cumbernauld.
When, after delays arising from the
movement of heavy artillery, the Prince and
Lord John joined forces, the Jacobite main
body numbered approximately 9,000 men –
the largest single force Charles would ever
field in the course of the conflict.

The city of Stirling surrendered to the
rebels on 8 January, but like Edinburgh
before it, Stirling's castle held out, its
position atop a steep rock rendering it
unassailable barring protracted siege
operations. Undaunted, the rebels dug
trenches in unforgiving earth replete with
stones, and struggled to mount guns with
the requisite trajectory to inflict any damage
on the impregnable position. Two days

earlier, Henry Hawley, now commander of government troops in Scotland, had arrived in the capital with impressive resources: a portion of Cumberland's forces tasked with pursuing the Jacobites across the English border, as well as most of the infantry drawn from Wade's command, originally at Newcastle. General Hawley had had a long and active career, having signed up as an ensign in 1694 and fought as a captain of dragoons in Spain. By the time of the rising of 1715 he was colonel of his regiment, at the head of which he was wounded at Sheriffmuir. In 1742, as a major-general, he accompanied Lord Stair to Holland and served as second-in-command of the cavalry

at Dettingen. He fought at Fontenoy in May 1745 and replaced Sir James Campbell when he was killed in action. In the course of the rebellion he would maintain order through harsh discipline and other severe measures, and was known as the 'chief justice' by his men for his regular practice of execution.

On 13 January Hawley dispatched cavalry under General Huske to reconnoitre the area and discover the rebels' position. Two days later the army's main body, with Hawley present, followed, in order to break the siege of Stirling.

The battle of Falkirk

The Jacobites learned of their opponents' presence on January 13, when scouts under Lord George Murray observed Hawley's van at Linlithgow. Rebel forces were recalled from their various concentrations in the vicinity of Stirling and assembled near Bannockburn, apart from a contingent of 1,200 who remained behind to continue their fruitless

Stirling Castle. The renewed siege of the fortress in the second half of January had achieved nothing apart from providing an opportunity for many Highlanders to desert, Murray appreciated the futility of continuing the siege as well as the danger of remaining static. He therefore recommended a retreat into the Highlands for the winter and an offensive against the Highland forts – a course of action to which the Prince gave his reluctant approval. (Author's collection)

The battle of Falkirk, 17 January 1746

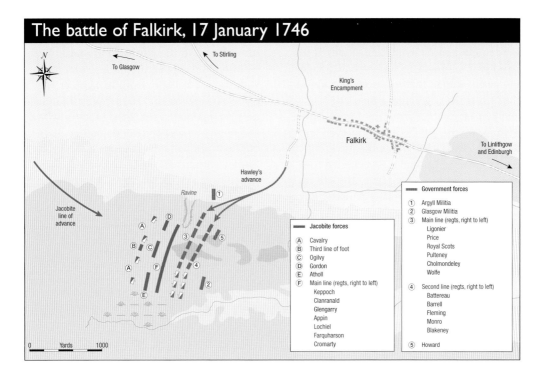

N

To Glasgow

To Stirling

King's Encampment

Falkirk

To Linlithgow and Edinburgh

Hawley's advance

Ravine

Jacobite line of advance

Jacobite forces

- (A) Cavalry
- (B) Third line of foot
- (C) Ogilvy
- (D) Gordon
- (E) Atholl
- (F) Main line (regts, right to left)
  - Keppoch
  - Clanranald
  - Glengarry
  - Appin
  - Lochiel
  - Farquharson
  - Cromarty

Government forces

- (1) Argyll Militia
- (2) Glasgow Militia
- (3) Main line (regts, right to left)
  - Ligonier
  - Price
  - Royal Scots
  - Pulteney
  - Cholmondeley
  - Wolfe
- (4) Second line (regts, right to left)
  - Battereau
  - Barrell
  - Fleming
  - Monro
  - Blakeney
- (5) Howard

0   Yards   1000

siege of the castle. On the 15th the Jacobites established themselves in line of battle on Plean Muir, six miles from Falkirk, and maintained their position for three days awaiting Hawley's approach. When government forces failed to appear, Lord George Murray ordered an advance to rising ground at Falkirk, within a mile of the government position.

Hawley had established himself with hollow and marshy ground to his front and several enclosures with water-filled ditches on his right. Murray decided to seize the Hill of Falkirk, an open ridge south-west of the town with a view of the government camp. They employed a deception plan which sent a column down a road in the opposite direction; although Hawley observed this he made no reconnaissance to establish the enemy's exact whereabouts, despite his considerable advantage in cavalry. Only at 1pm on January 17 did the government forces hear word of the rapid rebel advance, whereupon Hawley ordered the army to advance in a race to reach the summit of the hill before the enemy. Uneven ground confused the ranks and tired the men.

The rebels were deployed in three lines, with the first two of infantry, and the third of cavalry and a few French regulars. All told, the Jacobites numbered 5,800 infantry and 360 cavalry. Hawley's men were also arrayed in three lines, with the cavalry in the front. The general commanded about 5,500 infantry and 500 cavalry. Behind the dragoons were a further 700 loyal volunteers, deployed around houses and walls. More loyal troops, with a few companies of regulars – about 800 all told – stood behind the rear of Hawley's left.

Fighting began at 4pm when Hawley launched his dragoons in a frontal assault against one of Lord George Murray's Highland brigades. Rebel volleys did little damage but the charge halted, apart from a few troopers who reached the line and were driven off; soon the cavalry retreated towards the right, moving between the two opposing forces and taking fire from the remainder of the Jacobite line. One regiment rode back down the hill into a body of volunteers, who fired at them in protest. Delighted by their repulse of the cavalry, the rebel brigade launched an unauthorized counter-attack down the hill, chasing the dragoons and ploughing into a body of loyal militia. They were soon followed by the remainder of the Jacobite front line, which charged through the severe rainfall that was now blowing in the face of the government line. The majority of Hawley's men, tired from their advance up the hill, became unnerved and fled back down, though regiments on the right, protected by a ravine, remained firm and fired into the rebels' flank. The 4th then altered its front to face left, advanced against the rebels, and stopped to fire several volleys. The rebels ran off, taking the second line, also panicking, with them. Some of the Jacobites rallied and returned to the field, but this gave Hawley's troops time to launch a small cavalry attack against the rebels who remained on the hill. At the same time some of the government infantry were rallied with a view to a counter-attack, but poor visibility and the absence of a concentrated rebel force

on the field rendered this impossible. Moreover, when the Scots émigré infantry moved forward the government dragoons withdrew, taking the supporting infantry with them. On their return to camp Hawley's troops discovered that the artillery train had been abandoned, leaving the infantry to drag away one gun and recover two others later.

The storm had now become so severe that Hawley withdrew from his position and retired to the protection of Linlithgow. As a result of Hawley's abandonment of the field and the French occupying Falkirk with a few troops, the rebels could claim victory, in spite

The Castle of Doune, two miles north-west of Stirling, where Prince Charles left a small garrison and a group of prisoners after the battle of Falkirk. The significance of this well-built structure lay in its proximity to the Jacobites' access over the upper Forth, since the commanding position of Stirling Castle's guns prevented the rebels from crossing the city's bridge. (Author's collection)

of the fact that most of their own men had fled the field. They were unable to chase Hawley to Edinburgh and ultimately retreated north rather than risk another such encounter. Falkirk was a disorganized battle, fought before the second lines of both armies were properly deployed. This later contributed to utter confusion for both sides, who found themselves fighting amidst thunderous rain, wind and growing darkness. Both sides claimed victory, but the credit must go to the Jacobites, especially as it represented a serious psychological blow to the government. Neither side suffered many casualties: the rebels lost about 50 killed and 70 wounded, while government forces suffered around 70 killed and 200–300 missing.

The news of Hawley's setback caused considerable dismay. The King, in his recent speech to Parliament, had reassured the House of his confidence that, with large numbers of reinforcements sent to Scotland, the rebellion would soon be quelled. Prestonpans had not been an aberration; against all expectations, Falkirk confirmed that the Highlanders could still mount an impressive attack and at the very least fight government troops to a standstill. The humiliation took on all the greater significance when seen in light of the experience of the government troops, 12 battalions of which were veteran units, and nine of which had just returned from service in Flanders. Circumstances now demanded the presence of a new commander: the Duke of Cumberland, who had left Carlisle in order to take up command of forces meant to repel an invasion along the south coast. He now received orders to take command in Scotland to pursue the complete destruction of the Jacobite army.

William Augustus, Duke of Cumberland, was born the third son of George II. His parents had groomed him for the Navy, and though in 1740 Cumberland sailed on Sir John Norris' flagship, the young royal preferred a career in the Army. In April of the same year he became – naturally by purchase – colonel of the Coldstream Guards, transferring in February 1741 to the Grenadier Guards. In December, still only 20 and with virtually no military experience, Cumberland was promoted to major-general. It was in the worst traditions of an age in which a powerful combination of patronage and money virtually guaranteed that deserving and undeserving candidates would be promoted in unequal measure. However, in April 1743 he accompanied his father on campaign in Germany and showed great coolness under fire at Dettingen; there, wounded by a musket ball in his calf, he directed that the surgeon attend a more seriously wounded French officer before treating his own injury.

Promoted to lieutenant-general in June, his request for any command in the campaign of 1744 was initially refused, as the king preferred to appoint the Earl of Stair as commander-in-chief of British forces. When, however, Stair refused to serve under the Austrian marshal, Königsegg, the king arranged to have his son appointed. In March 1745 Cumberland was given the title of captain-general of British land forces both in Britain and overseas, a position dormant since Marlborough's time. He took command at Brussels on 10 April and a month later confronted the French at Fontenoy, where he personally led an infantry attack on the enemy centre. Heavily outnumbered, Cumberland was defeated, thus enabling the French to complete the conquest of Flanders by October. While the French were in winter quarters Cumberland, now grown quite corpulent and unmilitary in his bearing and yet still only 24 – the same age as his new nemesis Prince Charles – returned to Britain to confront the Jacobite threat.

Withdrawal north

Under other circumstances, the outcome of Falkirk ought to have pleased Charles and his followers, although it was of no tangible benefit to the cause of Stuart restoration. But it stood as only an incomplete victory which enabled Hawley to retreat without pursuit, thus preserving his forces in Scotland to

The Duke of Cumberland, who having failed to achieve a victory on the Continent against the French, delivered the *coup de grace* to the Jacobite rising at Culloden. He died at the age of 44, associated in Scotland with brutality and earning the nickname 'The Butcher' for his ruthless victimization of the Highland clans in the aftermath of the '45 rising. (National Army Museum)

fight another day. Charles returned to Bannockburn the day after Falkirk and his troops redoubled their efforts at taking Stirling Castle, where 1,200 men under the Duke of Perth struggled to make headway, in exchange for many lives lost from sniping

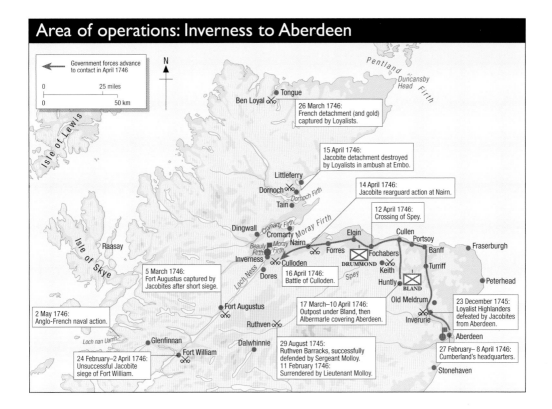

Area of operations: Inverness to Aberdeen

Government forces advance to contact in April 1746

0   25 miles
0   50 km

N

26 March 1746:
French detachment (and gold) captured by Loyalists.

15 April 1746:
Jacobite detachment destroyed by Loyalists in ambush at Embo.

14 April 1746:
Jacobite rearguard action at Nairn.

12 April 1746:
Crossing of Spey.

5 March 1746:
Fort Augustus captured by Jacobites after short siege.

16 April 1746:
Battle of Culloden.

2 May 1746:
Anglo-French naval action.

17 March–10 April 1746:
Outpost under Bland, then Albermarle covering Aberdeen.

23 December 1745:
Loyalist Highlanders defeated by Jacobites from Aberdeen.

24 February–2 April 1746:
Unsuccessful Jacobite siege of Fort William.

29 August 1745:
Ruthven Barracks, successfully defended by Sergeant Molloy.
11 February 1746:
Surrendered by Lieutenant Molloy.

27 February– 8 April 1746:
Cumberland's headquarters.

Place names: Pentland, Duncansby Head, Firth, Tongue, Ben Loyal, Isle of Lewis, Littleferry, Dornoch, Dornoch Firth, Tain, Dingwall, Cromarty Firth, Cromarty, Moray Firth, Elgin, Cullen, Portsoy, Banff, Fraserburgh, Raasay, Beauly Firth, Moray Firth, Nairn, Forres, Fochabers, Isle of Skye, Inverness, Culloden, DRUMMOND, Keith, Turriff, Peterhead, Dores, Spey, Huntly, BLAND, Loch Ness, Fort Augustus, Old Meldrum, Glenfinnan, Ruthven, Fort William, Dalwhinnie, Inverurie, Aberdeen, Loch nan Uamh, Stonehaven

and exhaustion as well as much valuable time. Many clan leaders began to advise lifting the siege and withdrawing north into the Highlands – thus avoiding the superior numbers of government forces now marching to the relief of Stirling – to establish winter quarters in the safety of the north, and ultimately seize the Highland forts. The Prince reluctantly agreed; indeed, he had little choice, for he appreciated that he had overruled his chiefs on numerous occasions in the course of the rebellion and could no longer dictate strategy in light of the sacrifices and mistakes already made.

The rebels began their retreat north on 1 February, marked by poor organization and disagreements over plans. At Crieff, a Council of War decided to divide the army and proceed north, with both elements to rendezvous at Inverness. The Prince's troops were to march over the Grampians along the military road, while Lord George would lead the Lowland troops along the coast road to Inverness via Angus and Aberdeen. Meanwhile, the Duke of Cumberland had

reached Edinburgh on 30 January, where he received an enthusiastic welcome. The 24-year-old veteran of Fontenoy did not dawdle. The army left the capital on the following morning, keen to discover the whereabouts of the rebel army and bring it to battle. For his part Charles was keen to convince his followers that his campaign was not to be a repetition of 1715–16, in which the Jacobites, after initial success, had retreated into the Highlands, only for the army to disperse and their leader return to France, his adherents to suffer the consequences.

Charles reached Inverness where, as elsewhere, a small force of local militia, regulars and volunteers held the stronghold – in this case Fort George, to the Highlanders a hated symbol of Hanoverian rule – against calls for surrender. The garrison lost heart and gave over the place on 20 February, whereupon the jubilant clansmen blew the structure to smouldering ruins. Lord George Murray had now arrived on the scene from Aberdeen, his troops freezing and exhausted.

Retreat of the Highlanders from Perth, February 1746. Following the failure of the Jacobite siege of Stirling and large-scale desertions, the rebels retreated into the Highlands for the winter, pursued by Cumberland until bad weather obliged him to halt at Perth on 6 February. (The Stapleton Collection/The Bridgeman Art Library)

The Duke of Cumberland, meanwhile, his forces burdened by an immense baggage train in the depth of winter and unable to keep pace with the rebels, decided to rest his men at Perth and await better marching conditions. Campaigning in the Highlands at this time of year posed a host of logistical problems which he was anxious to avoid. While the Duke remained at Perth, 5,000 Hessian mercenaries and other auxiliaries arrived in the Firth of Forth, meant to garrison Perth on the departure of Cumberland's forces for Aberdeen, their next objective. The Jacobites were not inactive; they captured Fort Augustus on 5 March and several weeks later the Duke of Perth put to flight the forces under Lord Loudoun. A group of loyal Argyllshire militia in Keith were taken prisoner, and Macpherson of Cluny and Lord George Murray conducted a brilliant thrust into Perthshire and besieged Blair Castle. But such operations were merely peripheral to the principal concern: the whereabouts of Cumberland's main army, about whose progress intelligence arrived at rebel headquarters on 12 April.

Cumberland's main army was now in Aberdeen; just over 80 miles from the Prince's in Inverness. The future of the Jacobite cause would now rest on the rebels' response. From all around, their forces answered orders to consolidate in anticipation of imminent battle.

Lord George Murray (1694–1760), Jacobite commander

Born near Perth, the sixth son of John Murray, 1st Duke of Atholl, and Lady Katherine Douglas, Lord George Murray attended Glasgow University in 1710 but left the following year to join the British Army as an ensign, serving in Flanders. During the rising of 1715 he was in Atholl and joined the Old Pretender's cause, together with two of his brothers – one of whom, William, Marquess of Tullibardine, commanded the Atholl Brigade in which Lord George served as a battalion commander. As he was raising recruits in Fife, Lord George was not present at the battle of Sheriffmuir and thus did not witness the defeat of the Atholl clansmen, who were on the Jacobite left wing. He and Tullibardine fled from South Uist to the Continent the following year, where Murray settled first at Avignon and later at Bordeaux. In 1719, he returned to Scotland where he served under his brother and the Earl Marischal, and was wounded at the battle of Glenshiel. He again sought refuge on the Continent, first in Holland and then in France, but secretly returned to Scotland in 1724 to visit his dying father. The following year the British government pardoned him for his part in the previous rebellions. He married in 1729 and settled on a comfortable living near Tullibardine Castle. Just prior to the 1745 Rebellion he held a post under General Cope, commander of government forces in Scotland, and in doing so – notwithstanding his subsequent loyal service to the Young Pretender – never entirely divested himself of the taint of suspicion in the eyes of some Jacobites, such as Colonel O'Sullivan, one of the Prince's chief advisers, with whom Murray frequently clashed during the campaign.

When the rebellion began Lord George left Cope's service, and joined the Prince near Perth on 3 September, while his brother (James Murray, 2nd Duke of Atholl) remained loyal to the Hanoverian crown. Lord George's devotion to the Stuart cause never appeared credible to many in the Prince's entourage, especially to his secretary, Murray of Broughton, and the increasingly regular disputes which arose between Lord George and the Prince over strategy did nothing to dispel such suspicions. Nevertheless, as a lieutenant-general he shared senior command, together with the Duke of Perth and his brother William, over Jacobite forces. At Prestonpans on 21 September Lord George commanded the left wing, making a significant contribution to the Jacobite victory by suggesting to the Prince that the army make use of the path through the morass so as to surprise Cope's army. On the eve of the battle, however, he was outraged to hear that Charles had deployed the Atholl Brigade without his consent. On the other hand, Lord George had conceived his own plans for the battle without consulting fellow officers or the Prince.

Lord George proved a sensible commander who recognized that, notwithstanding their high morale and eagerness for battle, Highland forces required at least a modicum of formal drill, a simple form of which he devised. During the campaign in England, he carefully managed the supply of provisions, resulting in a minimum of losses through illness as a consequence. He was known to pay particular attention to logistics, as he himself indicated in a post-war record of the campaign:

As I had formerly known something of a Highland army, the first thing I did was to advise the Prince to endeavour to get proper people for provisors [sic] and commissaries, for otherwise there would be no keeping the men together, and that they would straggle through the whole country upon their marches if it was left to themselves to find provisions, which, beside the inconveniency of irregular marches, and much

Lord George Murray, the principal commander of Jacobite forces in 1745–46. From the outset of the campaign he had a poor relationship with the Prince and his staff. Murray believed in the need to call occasional councils of war in which all commanders would be consulted and their opinions sought. The Prince, who believed himself entitled to act as circumstances required, found this method repugnant. (Priscus)

time lost, great abuses would be committed, which, above all things, we were to avoid.

His political judgement was poor at times. As a member of the Prince's council, he proposed excluding Catholics from this body as a propaganda device, intended to counteract the view of some that the Jacobite cause was principally a Catholic enterprise. He soon retracted his recommendation. On the other hand, his thoughts on strategy rested on sound principles. He expressed doubts on the wisdom of invading England, on the basis that the French were unlikely to send a large expedition to the south to aid this thrust, and refused to put faith in the notion of large-scale desertions from British ranks. His pessimistic attitude in general, marked by a concern that the rebellion would end in failure as it had 30 years before, further strained relations with Charles; this was exacerbated by Lord George's opposition to the Prince's intended abolition of the Act of Union.

At the outset of the campaign in England, Lord George again overruled the Prince on strategic matters – advocating a march to Carlisle via Cumberland rather than confronting Wade at Newcastle. Lord George's advocacy of the former plan enjoyed the support of most of his fellow senior officers and was in fact implemented, encouraging the gradual rift that was thereafter to characterize relations between the Prince and his commander. Lord George resigned briefly at Carlisle when the Prince suggested that the Duke of Perth, as a Catholic, should accept the city's capitulation, but upon resuming command, he continued to express his serious concerns over the wisdom of proceeding ever-further south. His apprehensions were allayed by Charles's contention that he possessed letters of support from English Jacobites promising to assemble at Preston.

Once the army reached Derby in early December, with no significant signs of discontent amongst the people or overt support for the Stuart claim – still less evidence of imminent French support – Lord George, regarding himself as having been misled by Charles's unsubstantiated assertions and unfounded optimism, determined to bring Jacobite forces back to Scotland, and gained increasing support among fellow officers against the minority who backed the Prince's strategy, such as the Duke of Perth. Whether or not the army could have reached London and defeated its garrison remains one of the great speculative questions of British military history. It is certain, however, that Murray was instrumental in bringing the southward march to an end, and this he conducted exceptionally well. Only at Clifton in December did government forces manage to overtake the Jacobite retreat, and in the event Lord George fought this rearguard action with minor casualties and extricated himself without Cumberland's superior numbers overwhelming him.

Murray's sound judgement continued to serve him well once the Jacobite army reached Scotland. He continued to insist that the Prince leave military matters to his commanders and rightly advised Charles to make use of his recently reinforced army to occupy the high ground at Falkirk, whence he achieved a technical defeat over Hawley. Still, he and the Prince continued to differ, particularly over Lord George's decision to retreat from Stirling, which Charles opposed. Serious disagreements arose at the last Council of War at Crieff on 2 February, after which the army continued its retreat. But even to the last, on the eve of Culloden Murray kept a sound head and sensibly recommended against deploying the army on the flat and boggy ground of Culloden Moor, only to be overruled by the Prince, who disapproved of Lord George's recall of the abortive late-night attack which formed the prelude to the battle itself.

At Culloden Murray commanded the right wing, where he led the attack that penetrated the government's first line and led to the capture of two guns before Murray was unhorsed. Pessimistic about the prospects of success even before the fighting had begun, he nevertheless did not lose heart when the first attack failed to drive off the opposing infantry, and returned briefly to the fray with more Highlanders in support. He rode off the field with the centre and right and the next day tendered his resignation at Ruthven, reproaching the Prince by letter. Charles had exaggerated his claims of eventual French support and ignored his advice about the unsuitability of Culloden Moor as a battleground.

In the aftermath of the disaster Lord George had no option but to seek refuge, which he took in Atholl. After eight months as a fugitive he sailed to Holland on 16 December 1746, with his treachery so confirmed as to deny him any possibility of rehabilitation and reconciliation with the Hanoverian establishment. At the same time, his wife and children were ejected from Tullibardine Castle by James, 2nd Duke of Atholl. For the next two years he journeyed through Italy and Germany, Poland and Holland before finally settling in Rome, where in 1747 he received support from James, the Old Pretender. Charles, embittered by what he regarded as Murray's treasonable conduct

Lord George Murray at Falkirk, 17 January 1746. He positioned his forces on high ground, obliging Hawley to attack uphill in the face of driving rain and high winds. After repulsing Hawley's dragoons, the Highlanders charged the enemy front line, driving off most of Hawley's infantry, apart from two regiments on the right wing which withdrew intact. Murray was unable to pursue owing to the indiscipline of his troops, thus allowing Hawley to regroup and retreat to Edinburgh. (Stuart Reid collection)

during the rebellion, refused to grant him an audience, despite which Lord George never abandoned his belief in the Jacobite cause. He died in Holland on 11 October 1760.

Much has been made of Lord George's apparent defeatism in the course of the 1745–46 campaign, his decision to turn back at Derby exemplifying his conservative approach to warfare. He had originally believed in consolidating the gains made in Scotland rather than launching an invasion of England, and thus did not see the reasoning for confronting Wade on English soil when that blow ought to be struck north of the border. Similarly, he demonstrated his caution by withdrawing after inflicting a serious blow at Falkirk when he might have exploited this success. In this respect he functioned as a competent, though by no means distinguished, commander. Had he pursued the Prince's objective and made for London the rebellion might have succeeded in taking the city, but with no appetite for a Stuart restoration amongst the English population and no substantial military force with which to capitalize on such temporary gains, long-term success appears extremely remote, giving due weight to Murray's pessimism about the whole affair and his insistence on turning back at Derby.

If he had his detractors, he appears to have displayed many of the qualities of a fine commander, working long hours and taking pains to draft and issue clear and effective orders. Attention to detail marked Lord George out from many of his contemporaries, for 18th-century officers justly deserved their reputation for poor administration and frivolous pursuits at the expense of their professional duties. In describing his role in a short post-war history of his part in the rebellion, he fairly reflected his style of leadership on campaign:

I was always early in the mornings employed in some necessary work: any thing that was readiest served for breakfast; and I commonly dined betwixt four and five, and no supper. Any body who had business with me, or any thing to say, had access at all hours, whether I were at meals or in bed. On some occasions, I have been waked six times a-night, and had either orders to write, or letters to answer, every time; for as I mostly commanded a separate body of the army, I had many details that, in a more regular army, would belong to different people. I not only wrote the orders myself when I commanded a separate corps of the army, or directed them, but to any officer that was to go upon a party, or upon an outpost, I endeavoured to explain every thing that might happen, and answered any objections that could be started, besides giving the orders in writing, by which means there was no mistake or confusion, and the officers did their duty with cheerfulness, and made their reports with exactness.

Even in an age of relatively 'civilized' warfare, in which European armies largely respected the lives of prisoners and civilians, the forces under Lord George Murray behaved exceptionally well, partly owing to the careful attention he paid to matters of discipline, particularly with respect to looting, though it must be acknowledged that numerous violations of his instructions explicitly condemning the practice occurred during the retreat to Scotland:

… above all, I was particularly careful to have discipline as exactly kept as was possible, and, to the utmost of my power, I protected the country wherever I went; and upon any complaints, I almost always got them redressed. The taking of horse for carrying their baggage, or for sick men, was what the Highlanders committed the greatest excess in. Many hundreds I got restored; and if the people whom they belonged to could but fix where they were, or who had them, I never failed to get them restored, though we were obliged to allow them to be carried a day or two's march, perhaps, longer than they should. As to plundering, our men were not entirely free of it; but there was much less of this than could have been expected, and few regular armies but are as guilty.

Various first-hand accounts also attest to his humane treatment of prisoners and the care he bestowed on the sick and wounded:

But in nothing was I more careful than about prisoners, even the common soldiers, when they were under my charge. I caused to take all the care possible of the sick and wounded. I had many letters, full of acknowledgments, from the officers… All those who were taken in Athol, were as civilly used as possible, so long as I had the care of them. I visited the soldiers that were prisoners in the church of Inverness, and got relief and assistance sent to the sick.

If Lord George Murray does not figure within the ranks of history's great commanders, a lengthier campaign, with a greater number of forces at his disposal, might yet have developed him into one of the more distinguished military leaders of the 18th century.

The battle of Culloden

By April 1746 the Jacobite army had passed its peak; it had suffered considerably from the trials of winter, its provisions were low and neither the Prince's treasury nor the private finances of his officers could do much to meet the desperate financial needs of the troops, whose pay by this time stood weeks in arrears. Nothing further could be gleaned from the Lowlands owing to its occupation by government forces, the Royal Navy was successfully blockaded the coast, choking off further supplies from the French, and many otherwise loyal clansmen began to return to their homes to plant spring crops. Nor could all the troops be recalled in time to meet Cumberland's offensive. Lochiel and Keppoch were busy besieging Fort William with their forces; others were in Badenoch; Simon Fraser, Lord Lovat was on a recruiting drive for his regiment and 700 other clansmen – Mackenzies, MacGregors and MacDonalds – were in Sutherland keeping an eye on Loudoun's dispersed units.

Given such dispositions, by some accounts at least a third and as much as a half of the Jacobite forces were not immediately available to the main army under the Prince and Lord George Murray. Nevertheless, if his army had endured a great deal of privation, the Prince believed they had achieved much, and consistent with his usual attitude of confident expectation – for which circumstances as never before comprehensively failed to justify – clung to the belief that his Highlanders could continue to overcome all adversity and accomplish ever-greater feats against an enemy whose forces stood superior to his own in all respects, except perhaps its senior leadership.

In contrast, when Cumberland's army left Aberdeen, making its way through Banff, it numbered 7,100 men, with reinforcements en route. On 14 April the army, now increased to a strength of 9,000, reached

Nairn, approximately 17 miles from Inverness. The following night the Jacobites attempted an abortive raid against government lines, but in the confusion and darkness nothing but exhaustion and demoralization prevailed, obliging the troops to return to their position on Culloden Moor, where on the 16th Cumberland advanced to make contact. The culminating act of the rebellion was now to be played out.

Culloden Moor is about half a mile wide, and in April 1746 there stood on it a walled enclosure, the Culwhiniac Parks, which ran from the Jacobite position right down to the river Nairn, with the Jacobite left anchored on the walls of Culloden Parks. The moor was quite wet, with pools of water and soft earth throughout. The rebels mustered around 3,800 infantry arrayed in their front line, with a second, reserve line of about 700. Their mounted force was perhaps 150. Their artillery, probably a dozen pieces in all, appears to have been distributed across the front rather than concentrated. Cumberland advanced from Nairn and deployed his forces

The battle of Culloden was the last battle fought on the soil of mainland Britain, and the Jacobite defeat marked the end of hopes for a Stuart restoration. (Mary Evans Picture Library)

The death of Major Gillies McBean of Lady Mackintosh's Regiment, which occupied a position in the Jacobite centre at Culloden. (The Bridgeman Art Library)

opposite the rebel position in three lines, with the front left anchored on Leanach and the walled enclosure to its front. Most of the cavalry was deployed on the left, in front of the Culwhiniac walls. Between the battalions 3-pounder guns were deployed and six mortars were placed between the first and second lines. Some changes took place before the action; when the rebels appeared to shift to the left, Cumberland moved forward some of his reserves to extend his right, including a portion of his cavalry, which stood well to the right of the infantry.

Action commenced when ten troops of Cumberland's cavalry and four companies of his loyal Highlanders, facing the walls of Culwhiniac Parks and finding they could not advance across this obstacle, were ordered by Major-General Humphrey Bland to demolish it so as to allow the passage of the cavalry.

Bland, the senior cavalry officer at Culloden, had spent much of his career in the dragoons. He served in several of Marlborough's campaigns, received a wound

at Almanara in 1710, and had his horse shot from under him at the battle of Dettingen in 1743 and distinguished himself at Fontenoy two years later. While lieutenant-colonel of the King's Regiment of Horse, later the King's Dragoon Guards, he wrote his *Treatise on Discipline*, which the government released in numerous editions and which for much of the 18th century was the standard textbook of Army drill and discipline, replacing the obsolete 50-year-old treatise by the Earl of Orrey. It covered the tactics employed in Marlborough's campaigns as well as methods of maintaining discipline in the field.

Bland had earlier recognized that the Culwhiniac enclosure was unoccupied and therefore the Jacobite right could be outflanked by passing through it. Cumberland's loyal Highlanders thus pulled down part of the front and rear walls, which not only increased the chance of victory but also threatened to sever the rebel line of retreat across the river Nairn. The cavalry and Highlanders duly moved into the empty enclosure, an event witnessed by the rebel right which was too far away to do anything about it; Lord George Murray had refused to heed advice before the battle that such a threat ought to be avoided by posting some men within the enclosure.

On passing through the south wall the government forces halted before a ditch, slightly behind the rebel right. The rebels thereupon redeployed units from their line to face them while other battalions from the reserve moved off to the right to their assistance. Hawley now made the mistake of choosing to retain his Highlanders in an enclosure rather than deploy them with the dragoons, for reasons which have never been made clear. Hawley and Bland then advanced with the cavalry across a stream, which flowed on a parallel course with the rear wall of Culwhiniac Parks, and turned north to face the rebel infantry which had altered its front to protect the exposed rebel rear. A small force of Jacobite horsemen also confronted the government cavalry, together with several battalions of rebel infantry. These unexpected reinforcements made

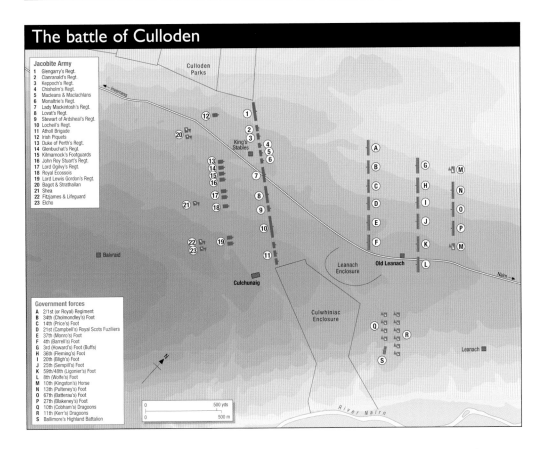

The battle of Culloden

Jacobite Army
1 Glengarry's Regt.
2 Clanranald's Regt.
3 Keppoch's Regt.
4 Chisholm's Regt.
5 Macleans & Maclachlans
6 Monaltrie's Regt.
7 Lady Mackintosh's Regt.
8 Lovat's Regt.
9 Stewart of Ardsheal's Regt.
10 Lochiel's Regt.
11 Atholl Brigade
12 Irish Piquets
13 Duke of Perth's Regt.
14 Glenbuchat's Regt.
15 Kilmarnock's Footguards
16 John Roy Stuart's Regt.
17 Lord Ogilvy's Regt.
18 Royal Ecossois
19 Lord Lewis Gordon's Regt.
20 Bagot & Strathallan
21 Shea
22 Fitzjames & Lifeguard
23 Elcho

Government forces
A 2/1st (or Royal) Regiment
B 34th (Cholmondley's) Foot
C 14th (Price's) Foot
D 21st (Campbell's) Royal Scots Fuziliers
E 37th (Monro's) Foot
F 4th (Barrell's) Foot
G 3rd (Howard's) Foot (Buffs)
H 36th (Fleming's) Foot
I 20th (Bligh's) Foot
J 25th (Sempill's) Foot
K 59th/48th (Ligonier's) Foot
L 8th (Wolfe's) Foot
M 10th (Kingston's) Horse
N 13th (Pulteney's) Foot
O 67th (Batterau's) Foot
P 27th (Blakeney's) Foot
Q 10th (Cobham's) Dragoons
R 11th (Kerr's) Dragoons
S Ballimore's Highland Battalion

a government advance much more difficult, and the initial advantage of surprise was partially spoiled by a lack of infantry support. Hawley therefore chose not to attack.

At about 1pm the rebels began firing their artillery, which however only inflicted light casualties on the government troops. Cumberland returned fire almost immediately and after about 15 minutes the Jacobite ranks grew restless, having lost over 100 men in the bombardment. Joseph Yorke, one of Cumberland's aides, observed that, 'When our cannon had fired about two rounds, I could plainly perceive that the rebels fluctuated extremely, and could not remain long in the position they were then in without running away or coming down upon us; and according as I thought, in two or three minutes they broke from the centre in three large bodies...' The Highlanders then charged at the run, many breaking the cohesion of their ranks and casting aside their muskets in favour of their swords. Most

of the attackers made headlong for the extreme government left, in the course of which several units became intermingled and order was lost, as Yorke noted further:

They broke from the centre in three large bodies, like wedges, and moved forward. At first they made a feint, as if they would come down upon our right, but seeing that wing so well covered, and imagining that they might surround the left because they saw no cavalry to cover it, two of these wedges bore down immediately upon Barrell's and Monroes regiments, which formed the left of the first line; and after firing very irregularly at a considerable distance, they rushed furiously in upon them, thinking to carry all before them, as they had done on former occasions.

Several hundred of these attackers fell to canister fire, while three battalions on the government left fired volleys at 50 yards and again at point-blank range. An anonymous corporal of Monro's regiment recorded that the Jacobite Highlanders advanced so swiftly that the defending infantry had only time to loose off two volleys:

... they [the Jacobites] began to play their Cannon very briskly upon us; but as soon as we saw them pointed, we stoop'd down, and the Balls flew over our Heads. Two Pieces of our Cannon play'd from our Left to their Right, which kill'd many of them, and made their whole body determine to come down upon our Left, compos'd of Barrel's, Monro's, and the Scots Fusiliers. When we saw them coming towards us in great Haste and Fury, we fired at about 50 Yards Distance, which made hundreds Fall; notwithstanding which, they were so numerous, that they still advanced, and were almost upon us before we had loaden again. We immediately gave them another full Fire...

For the Jacobites some consolation for defeat could be found in the individual heroic acts performed at the battle of Culloden, but ultimately, the wild charge – their only tactic in battle – did not suffice against infantry properly drilled in musketry and the use of the bayonet. (Mary Evans Picture Library)

The rebels in the centre and on the left nevertheless reached the government line, striking part of Monro's 37th and the leftmost regiment, Barrell's 4th. A fierce hand-to-hand action ensued in which the Jacobites suffered severe losses, proving at least the equality, if not the superiority, of musket and bayonet over broadsword and shield. One witness recorded that:

... the best of the clans ... made their strongest efforts to break them, but without effect, for the old Tangierines [Barrell's regiment] bravely repulsed these boasters, with a dreadful slaughter, and convinced them that the broad sword and target is unequal to the musket and bayonet, when in the hands of veterans, who are determined to use them – After the battle there was not a bayonet in this regiment but was either bloody or bent.

Barrell's finally broke when the rebels wrapped around its flanks and took two guns, upon which they continued into Monro's, which held the rebels back with the bayonet and several volleys. Both sides suffered great losses and the government line might have been broken had not the fierce resistance of these two regiments given General Huske time to organize a counter-attack with four fresh regiments, one under the command of James Wolfe, the future conqueror of Quebec. Some of the government infantry could bring flanking fire against the attackers and a series of close-range volleys from these 1,200 reinforcements devastated the closely packed rebel ranks, which had no effective means of reply. Thus, despite punching a hole in the government line, the Jacobites could not exploit this temporary advantage in the face of such destructive firepower.

The rebel left meanwhile advanced at a much slower pace, held up by marshy ground and pools of water, some a foot deep. Once the rebel Highlanders came into range of Cumberland's musketry they halted, and despite encouragement from their officers they would advance no further, choosing instead to discharge their pistols and wave

Culloden. For many clan chiefs the rebellion represented a means of holding back the forces of political and social change which threatened their ancient privileges and way of life. The outcome of Culloden brought a decisive end to all such aspirations. (Mary Evans Picture Library)

their swords. Those rebels who had not foundered in the boggy ground and managed to continue their advance were shot down as they approached the government position. Thus, the Jacobite left never reached Cumberland's line and government casualties in this sector were virtually nil. Murray, seeing the crisis at hand, now brought forward two regiments from his second line, but by then the battle was obviously lost. The rebel right wing broke first, followed shortly afterwards by the left when Cumberland, sensing the Jacobites' imminent collapse, ordered a cavalry charge with two troops of dragoons which hit the rebel flank and caused a general rout. James Johnstone, on the Prince's staff, rapidly looked for a means of escape:

I remained for a time motionless, and lost in astonishment; then, in a rage, I discharged my blunderbuss and pistols at the enemy and immediately endeavoured to save myself like the rest... I neither saw the Prince, nor his servants, nor anyone on horseback. They had all gone off and were already out of sight. I saw nothing but the most horrible of all spectacles; the field of battle, from the right to the left of our army covered with Highlanders dispersed and flying as fast as they could to save themselves.

The token French force, finding all was lost, offered brief resistance before surrendering, with over 100 casualties suffered at the hands of the dragoons. Other French infantry, on the rebel right, fought briefly until driven from the wall of Culchunaig. These and others fell prey to several squadrons of dragoons under Bland, which Hawley ordered to charge. Cumberland issued the order of 'no quarter', confirming a reputation for brutality which had yet to reveal its worst features. The cavalry swept the field, pursuing the fleeing Jacobites and cutting down large numbers, including many who gave over their weapons in token of surrender. One government officer commented how 'the moor was covered with blood; and our men, what with killing the

Culloden, the final act of a remarkable period of British history. Charles may have believed his bid for the throne had ended with his failure to penetrate further into England. His *coup de main* was extraordinary, but it had reached its high water mark at Derby and went no further. His hopes for widespread support from English Jacobites were dashed and, as for external support, France had failed to provide anything more than token assistance and in so doing denied the rebellion the vital aid it required. (National Army Museum)

enemy, dabbling their feet in the blood; and splashing it about one another, looked like so many butchers.'

The battle had lasted only 40 minutes, fought on the Jacobite side entirely by the Highlanders, for none of the Lowland regiments in the second line participated in the fighting, instead covering the retreat of those repulsed in the charge. About 2,000 Jacobites were killed, wounded and taken prisoner, of which about half died in action on the moor or in the retreat to Inverness. Cumberland lost around 50 killed and 250 wounded – a negligible loss. The defeat of the Jacobites does not appear surprising given the difficulties both on the day and the previous night. Indeed, the enthusiasm they displayed at Culloden, under the circumstances, is all the more

part in the fighting. In Cumberland's army, two regiments in the first line, two in the second, and one in reserve, plus most of the Campbells, never fired a shot. Government forces paid a small price for their victory, whereas practically every Highlander who had fought in the front rank of his respective regiment was killed, either in the charge or when caught between enemy ranks which closed behind them, allowing the next rank to shoot down those who partly penetrated Cumberland's line.

It is perhaps appropriate here to note how Culloden has left in its wake certain persistent myths which ought to be dispelled. Culloden is still sometimes seen as a battle fought exclusively between English and Scots when this is certainly not the case. Of Cumberland's 15 regular regiments, three were Scottish; in addition, the companies of Lord Loudoun's regiment and those of the Duke of Argyll's militia were Scots as well. Nor is it the case that the worst atrocities committed after the battle were on the orders of English officers, for Lowland Scots were at least as responsible.

On the morning following the battle, the right wing of the Jacobite army joined Macpherson of Cluny with no more than 400 men of his clan near Loch Moy. Lord George Murray dispatched a messenger to the Prince, then at Gorthlick, about 20 miles away, informing him of the grim situation: he had the bulk of the army with him – about 1,500 men, most suffering from acute hunger – and that only Macpherson and Ardshiel could be accounted for among the chiefs. Stocks of food at Ruthven were poor, for despite Lord George's strenuous efforts to ensure that meal be sent to Badenoch in the event of a defeat, nothing in fact arrived.

Nevertheless, Culloden did not crush the hopes of all Jacobites, some of whom regarded it as a redeemable failure. At Ruthven in Badenoch, between 1,500 and 1,800 men gathered, together with the Duke of Perth, the Marquess of Tullibardine, Lord George Murray and Lord John Drummond, who collectively expressed a desire to carry

remarkable when all evidence pointed towards defeat. One could argue that Culloden was a foregone conclusion, for only a portion of Cumberland's army was required to bring the Jacobite forces to heel. Lochiel, for instance, struck by musket balls in both ankles, continued to encourage his men forward. MacDonald of Keppoch fell after two shots, but did so with sword and musket held high in defiance.

The numbers actually engaged at Culloden were quite small, for despite the presence of approximately 14,000 troops on the field, probably no more than 3,000 actually took

Atrocities committed by Cumberland's troops after the battle of Culloden. Summary executions carried out by government troops accounted for the Jacobites carrying away as many of their wounded from the field as possible. Those left behind became the victims of looters and often met their end at the hands of enemy soldiers who went on to commit indiscriminate murder against the local population. Pursuing cavalry meted out great destruction against the fleeing rebels, most of whom received no quarter. (Author's collection)

on the fight. Within days a group of chiefs declared their willingness to raise further forces, reorganize those already under arms and renew the struggle.

The Prince, viewing the situation in a different light, believed the rebellion had collapsed and issued his last order, failing to accompany it with any words of gratitude for the sacrifices his followers had made: 'Let every man seek his own safety as best he can,' he declared, leaving Lord George Murray and Lord John Drummond to convey these sentiments. Chevalier de Johnstone recorded the break-up of the Jacobite forces:

Our separation at Ruthven was truly affecting. We bade one another an eternal adieu. No one could tell whether the scaffold would not be his fate. The Highlanders gave vent to their grief in wild howlings and lamentations; the tears flowed down their cheeks when they thought that their country was now at the discretion of the Duke of Cumberland, and on the point of being plundered; whilst they and their children would be reduced to slavery, and plunged, without resource into a state of remediless distress.

A good deal of bitterness was expressed by those officers who by their service to the Prince now found themselves in dreadful straits. They and thousands of others had risked everything on an enterprise which while most of them regarded from the beginning as unlikely to succeed, arose for the most part out of virtuous principle – loyalty to their monarch, a wish for an independent Scotland and an end to government corruption in Edinburgh.

Flora MacDonald (1722–90), Jacobite heroine

Flora MacDonald, a heroine of the Jacobite cause and a figure of romance, whose story has often veered into the fanciful thanks to the growth of legend and a series of imaginative biographers, was born into a Presbyterian household of modest means on the island of South Uist. Her father, the leaseholder of Milton and Bailvinach on the island, was a cousin of the chief of the MacDonalds of Clanranald and a relation of the Argyll Campbells. Her mother held connections with the MacDonalds of Sleat, the Lords of the Isles. Flora was known as a talented singer and dancer, and fond of playing the spinet, a type of small piano popular in the 18th century.

In 1745, she lived in Armadale in Skye with her mother and stepfather, her father having died 18 years before. Here she had no direct experience of the rebellion, for the chief of Sleat declined to lend his support to the Prince; indeed, he actively supported the government, recruiting an independent militia unit in which Flora's stepfather served as a captain. Her association with the rebellion emerged only after Culloden in April 1746 when the Prince went into hiding on South Uist, the home of her brother and the principal local clan, the Clanralds, who sympathized with the Jacobite cause. No sooner had the government received intelligence that Charles had fled to the Outer Hebrides than troops arrived to conduct a thorough search of the islands, on one occasion nearly apprehending him. The Prince eluded capture by fleeing inland with only two companions, hiding in a shieling (a shepherd's hut) near Ormaclett on the west coast of Uist. There the Prince's friends developed a plan to smuggle him back to Skye in the disguise of an Irish maid in Flora's employ. She remained ignorant of this plan until the night of 20 June, when

Prince Charles on the run, aided by Flora MacDonald. (Author's collection)

the Prince arrived in secret at a hut on a summer pasture on Sheaval Hill, where Flora was working for her brother as a shepherdess. To the Prince's request for assistance Flora gave her reluctant assent.

In all probability her stepfather planned the manner of Charles's escape, for as commander of the militia he ordered the release of Flora and Neil MacEachain, a kinsman posing as Flora's manservant, whom the militia arrested while trying to cross the ford between South Uist and Benbecula. The Prince, posing as 'Betty Burke', an Irish 'maid-servant', then proceeded across country alive with government troops, walking with two companions to the head of Loch Skipport where he boarded a small

fishing boat and crossed to the island of Wiay.
The next day he was rowed across to
Benbecula and arrived at Rossinish under
cover of darkness. With soldiers ubiquitous
in the area, the Prince and his companions
took shelter for three nights in a barn.
He and Flora then sailed in a small boat
from Benbecula to Skye on the night of
28–29 June, with the Prince disguised in
women's clothes, including shoes and
stockings, and a wig and cap which concealed
all but his face. Describing herself in the third
person, Flora recalled the incident:

*Miss MacDonald desired him [the Prince] to
dress himself in his new attire, which was soon
done; and, at a proper time, they removed their
quarters, and went near the water, with their
boat afloat nigh at hand, for readiness to
embark in case of any alarm from the shore.
Here they arrived very wet and wearied, and
made a fire upon a rock, to keep them somewhat*

*warm till night. They were soon greatly alarmed
by seeing four wherries full of armed men
making towards shore, which made them
extinguish their fire quickly, and to conceal
themselves amongst the heath. The wherries,
however, sailed by, without ever stopping, to the
southward, within a gun-shot of the spot where
they were lying among the heath.*

In the absence of wind they had to row
north-east along the coast until a westerly
breeze arose late in the evening, enabling
them to reach the north-western tip of
Skye some time before dawn. Flora recounts
the story:

*Next morning, Sunday, June 29th, the
boatmen knew not where they were, having no
compass, and the wind varying several times, it
being then again calm. However, at last they
made to the point of Waternish, in the west
corner of Sky, where they thought to have landed,*

Flora MacDonald, the most famous of the many Jacobite sympathizers who, at the risk of their lives and the confiscation of their properties, aided the Prince during his five months eluding the authorities in the Highlands and Western Isles. (Scottish National Portrait Gallery, Edinburgh/The Bridgeman Art Library)

but found the place possessed by a body of forces, who had three boats or yawls near the shore. One on board one of the boats fired at them to make them bring to, but they rowed away as fast as they could, being all the chance they had to escape, because there were several ships of war within sight. They got into a creek, or rather clift in a rock, and there remained some short time to rest the men, who had been all night at work, and to get their dinners of what provisions they had along with them. As soon as they could they set forwards again, because, as the militia could not bring them to, they had sent up to alarm a little town not far off. It was very lucky for them that it was a calm then, for otherwise they must inevitably have perished, or have been taken.

But their point of embarkation, Waternish Point, was the country of the MacLeods, a clan loyal to the government. When troops hailed their boat and ordered it ashore, the occupants ignored them and drew fire, though without receiving injury. They sailed across Loch Snizort and landed at Trotternish, near Mugstot (now Monkstadt) House, the seat of MacDonald of Sleat.

Lady Margaret MacDonald, wife of the chief who was away at the time at Fort Augustus with his independent company, provided the two with food, until a detachment of militia under Captain Alexander MacLeod of Bracadale arrived and took up residence in the house. Flora distracted this officer while the Prince was assisted by Alexander MacDonald of Kingsburgh, a friend of Lady Margaret's, to proceed south to MacDonald's residence. In the meantime, Lady Margaret and Flora dined with Captain MacLeod.

The following day Flora met up with the Prince and, together with MacDonald of

Prince Charles bidding adieu to his friends along the shores of Loch nan Uamh on 20 September 1746. Two French ships, the *Prince de Conti* and *L'Heureux*, left amidst the cover of early morning mist, taking aboard the Prince and a few adherents. (Author's collection)

Kingsburgh and MacEachain, trudged across country and reached Kingsburgh House where they received much-needed food and rest. Late the following day they proceeded to Portree, the Prince taking a less conspicuous route while Flora used the main road with MacEachain. Before dawn on 1 July, Charles said his farewell to Flora and crossed to Raasay before continuing on to the mainland, where after a further stint in hiding he left Scotland forever aboard a French ship which had managed to elude the many Royal Navy ships endeavouring to prevent the Prince's escape. In the meantime, Flora was given a cover story to allay the suspicions of those working assiduously for the Prince's apprehension.

Flora related these circumstances, again in the third person, shortly after the rebellion:

Miss MacDonald took leave of the Prince at Portree, and from thence went to her mother, after a fatiguing journey across the country. She never told her mother, or indeed any body else, what she had done. About eight or ten days after, she received a message from one of her own name, Donald MacDonald, of Castleton, in Sky, who lived about four miles from Slate, or Armadale, to come to his house, an officer of an independent company (one MacLeod of Taliskar) having desired him so to do. She, a little suspicious of what might happen, thought proper to consult some of her friends what she should do in the matter. They unanimously agreed she ought not to go, at least till next day; but go she would. Then she was instructed what to say upon an examination; and, accordingly, when that happened, she said she had seen a great lusty woman, who came to the boat side, as she was going on board, and begged to have a passage, saying she was a soldier's wife. Her request was granted; and, when she landed in Sky, she went away, thanking Miss for her favour; Miss adding withal, that she knew nothing of what became of her afterwards.

But no testimony could protect her now, for when the boatmen responsible for conveying Charles to Skye returned to Uist the authorities arrested them and discovered Flora's whereabouts. Taken aboard HMS *Furnace* Flora never revealed sufficient information to assist the authorities in locating the Prince. Although treated well, she was transferred to London aboard the *Bridgewater* and held in confinement, together with other prisoners of note, until shortly after the government announced a general amnesty in July 1746. Generously furnished with funds from a Jacobite sympathizer, Flora then travelled to Edinburgh, where she spent the winter of 1746–47 before returning to Skye in the summer. She married Allan MacDonald, a kinsman, in November 1750 and resided on a farm at Flodigarry before moving to Sleat. Flora raised seven children there until she and her husband fell on hard times, as a consequence of which in 1774 they emigrated to America, settling at Cheek's Creek, North Carolina, a place already inhabited by some of their relations.

When the American Revolution began the following year, the MacDonalds counted themselves within the loyalist camp; as such, her husband, son, and son-in-law all served in a loyalist Highland regiment which, defeated by the rebels at the battle of Moore's Creek Bridge on 27 February 1776, left Flora's husband Allan in captivity until his exchange for a rebel officer 18 months later. After much suffering during the civil war which had raged in the Carolinas during her husband's absence, Flora received permission from rebel authorities to travel to New York in April 1778 to see her husband. Upon his release he rejoined his regiment in Nova Scotia, but Flora, her health weakened and yearning for home, returned to Scotland in 1779 and settled on Skye, to where her husband also finally returned in 1785, when he found his back-pay for service in the war insufficient to cover the expense of starting a new life in Nova Scotia. The couple lived comfortably, thanks to the wealth accrued by one of their sons, at Penduin on Skye, where Flora died on 4 March 1790.

Highland life in the mid-18th century

To the English and to most Lowland Scots, the Highlands of Scotland were a remote and backward place populated by semi-barbaric peoples speaking an unintelligible language, who wore animal hides or lengths of patterned cloth, and who continued practices long since abandoned in the more civilized south: vendetta killings, feuds, forays, and cattle-stealing. If the English – with the Highlands 400 miles from London – were clearly ignorant of the Highlanders, even their near-neighbours, the Lowlanders, viewed them with suspicion and sometimes fear. Duncan Forbes, Lord President of the Court of Session, the government's adviser on Highland affairs, described the area thus:

What is properly called the Highlands of Scotland is that large tract of mountainous Ground to the Northwest of the Forth and the Tay, where the natives speak the Irish language. The inhabitants stick close to their antient and idle way of life; retain their barbarous customs and maxims; depend generally on their Chiefs as their Sovereign Lords and masters; and being accustomed to the use of Arms, and inured to hard living, are dangerous to the public peace; and must continue to be so until, being deprived of Arms for some years, they forget the use of them.

Dr Beattie, quoted by Daniel Defoe, described the harsh landscape that produced such a forbidding people:

… picturesque, but, in general, a melancholy country. Long tracts of mountainous desert, covered with dark heath, and often obscured by misty weather; narrow vallies thinly inhabited, and bounded by precipices, resounding with the fall of torrents; a soil so rugged, and a climate so dreary, as, in many parts, to admit neither the amusements of pasturage, nor the labours of agriculture; the mournful dashing of waves along the firths and lakes that intersect the country; the portentous noises which every change of the wind, and every encrease and diminution of the waters, are apt to raise in a lonely region full of echoes, and rocks, and caverns; the grotesque and ghastly appearance of such a landscape by the light of the moon: objects like these diffuse a gloom over the fancy, which may be compatible enough with occasional and social merriment, but cannot fail to tincture the thoughts of a native in the hour of silence and solitude.

The Highlanders lived a feudal existence based on a tribal system dating back hundreds of years, with ties of blood, name, loyalty and centuries of shared experience in close-knit communities which inexorably bound the members of the clan together. It was a way of life rendered the more powerful by its characteristic features: its distinctive language, music, formidable geography, and military traditions, all of which provided the region and its people with a strong identity not found anywhere else in Britain. While the Age of Enlightenment swept across England and the Scottish Lowlands, the Highlands, virtually frozen in medieval isolation, still awaited the onslaught of modernity. Thus, unsurprisingly, what passed for sophistication in the Lowlands equated to weakness and effeminacy in the mountains of the North, where the Highlanders looked down upon their southern neighbours as a corrosive influence, as Dr Samuel Johnson related in his account of the region:

By their Lowland neighbours they would not willingly be taught [English]; for they have long considered them as a mean and degenerate race. These prejudices are wearing fast away; but so much of them still remains, that when I asked a

Highland landscape. During his travels Daniel Defoe described the region thus: 'The pass into the *Highlands* is awfully magnificent: high, craggy, and often naked mountains present themselves to view, approach very near each other, and in many parts are fringed with wood, overhanging and darkening the [River] Tay, which rolls with great rapidity beneath… As the country is rough and uncultivated, the inhabitants are an hardy race of men, who make excellent soldiers … and I must add, that they are much [more] civilized to what they were formerly.' (© The Fleming-Wyfold Art Foundation/The Bridgeman Art Library)

very learned minister in the islands, which they considered as their most savage clans: 'Those,' said he, 'that live next [to] the Lowlands.'

By mid-century such attitudes were undergoing change – partly owing to the military roads built by Wade between 1726 and 1737, which allowed greater access of people and ideas to a most inaccessible region, and partly by the slow influence of the political and social changes occurring to the south.

Not every outsider regarded Highlanders with unmixed contempt. A Mr Pennant, whom Defoe quotes in his travel journal, found Highlanders

… indolent to a high degree, unless roused to war, or to any animating amusement; or, I may say from experience, to lend any disinterested assistance to the distressed traveller, either in directing him on his Way, or affording their aid in passing the dangerous torrents of the Highlands. They are hospitable to the highest degree, and full of generosity; are much affected with the civility of strangers, and have in themselves natural politeness and address, which often flows from the meanest [i.e. lowest socially] when least expected… They are excessively inquisitive after your business, your name, and other particulars of little consequence to them. They are most curious after the politics of the world, and when they can procure an old newspaper, will listen to it [read to them] with … avidity… They have much pride, and consequently are impatient of affronts, and revengeful of injuries; are decent in their general behaviour, inclined to superstitions, yet attentive to the duties of religion, and are capable of giving a most distinct account of their faith.

Nothing more readily marked out a Highlander than his appearance. An observer named Edward Burt, quoted by Defoe, described their peculiar form of dress:

The common habit of the Highlander is far from being acceptable to the eye. With them a small part of the plaid, which is not so large as the former, is set in folds and girt round the waist to make of it a short petticoat that reaches halfway down the thigh, the rest is brought over the shoulders and fastened before, below the neck often with a fork, and sometimes with a bodkin or sharpened piece of stick, so that they make pretty nearly the appearance of the poor women of London when they bring their gowns over their heads to shelter themselves from the rain. This dress is called the quelt [kilt], and for the most part they wear the petticoat so very short that in a windy day, going up a hill, or stooping, the indecency of it is plainly discovered.

To understand this society, one must understand the social structure of the clan, which Forbes described as

    ... a set of men all bearing the same sirname, and believing themselves to be related the one to the other, and to be descended from the same common stock. In each clan there are several subaltern tribes, who own their dependence on their own immediate chiefs but all agree in owing allegiance to the Supreme Chief of the Clan or Kindred and look upon it to be their duty to support him at all adventures.

The chief effectively dispensed justice and interpreted the law that governed his clan, which meant that, like in so many remote communities with ancient traditions, nothing like proper government jurisdiction permeated into their region. As a consequence, enforcement of the law had long since devolved upon the clan chiefs, in whose hands the distant government placed any hopes for a civilizing influence in an otherwise barbaric community. What the authorities could not achieve themselves, they deduced, might be achieved through intermediaries. 'It has been for a great many years impracticable (and hardly thought safe to try it)' Forbes observed,

Hard times. If the Highlands are ruggedly beautiful, in the 18th century they provided only the barest of subsistence for much of the impoverished population. During his tour of the area Dr Samuel Johnson said of it: 'Regions mountainous and wild, thinly inhabited, and little cultivated, make a great part of the earth, and he that has never seen them, must live unacquainted with much of the face of nature, and with one of the great scenes of human existence.' (© Oldham Gallery/The Bridgeman Art Library)

to give the Law its course among the mountains. It required no small degree of Courage, and a greater degree of power than men are generally possessed of, to arrest an offender or debtor in the midst of his Clan. And for this reason it was that the Crown in former times was obliged to put Sheriffships and other Jurisdictions in the hands of powerful families in the Highlands, who by their respective Clans and following could give execution to the Laws within their several territories, and frequently did so at the expense of considerable bloodshed.

Long before, the Crown had ennobled many chiefs, who became the unofficial agents of the law and royal authority, over time extending their wealth and power through increased landholdings and more tenants – and thus more men-at-arms – which was consistent with the feudal traditions which had long since ended in the rest of Britain. Indeed, clan chiefs effectively operated as laws unto themselves, with one oft-repeated anecdote confirming the fact.

    A woman stood accused of stealing money from the chief of her clan, MacDonald of Clanranald. It would not have occurred to anyone to take her before a court in Inverness or anywhere else for that matter; the chief condemned her to death by ordering her hair to be tied to seaweed among the rocks along the coast. In due course the tide rose and drowned her. With the chief the unquestioned master of the clan, a crime committed against him amounted to a crime committed to the clan as a whole, and hence no dissent arose. He also wielded enough power to burn the roof of a recalcitrant clansman's sod-and-roundstone cottage, especially if he refused to answer the call to arms, or he could banish convicted members of his clan to indentured servitude in Canada or America.

Burt, something of an amateur sociologist, identified the unique relationship between clansmen and their chief:

The ordinary Highlanders esteem it the most sublime degree of virtue to love their chief and pay him a blind obedience although it be in opposition to the government, the laws of the kingdom, or even the law of God. He is their idol; and as they profess to know no king but him…so will they say they ought to do whatever he commands.

But if the chief dispensed justice, he also protected his people and took a strong, paternalistic interest in their welfare. The loyalties between chief and clansmen were mutual, and this created the cohesive bond that rendered the clan a powerful communal institution. The chief's responsibilities ran to officiating disputes over property and other issues, for which he sometimes consulted with leading members of the clan. Notwithstanding his powerful position as landlord, judge, military commander and father of the tribe, he seldom ruled absolutely.

Officially, Highland chiefs did not owe their authority to the principle of hereditary right; but over the centuries this largely became the de facto situation. Where once, back in the mists of time, the land was communally owned, by the mid-18th century it was the chief's – not by virtue of a deed, but by the clan's tacit recognition that by

tradition he occupied the top rung of the hierarchy. This and other aspects of the Highland social system had remained intact for centuries, such as the mystic bond between unrelated male infants sharing the same mother's milk. The son of a chief was often wet-nursed by a woman of lower status within the clan, a tradition which bound the boy by honour to that woman's own son, whereby, in boyhood, each pledged to defend the life of the other, even while wide social divisions separated their respective families.

Beneath the clan chief lay a host of various officials, with tenants beneath them. The wealthier of these tenants managed land held under 'tacks' or leases, which the chief granted them as subordinate landlords. These 'tacksmen', though unrelated to the chief himself, nevertheless played an important part in Highland society, and in time of emergency a tacksman's status enabled him to occupy a higher place in the clan regiment – serving as a junior officer or senior NCO – than the humbler tenants working the land. Needless to say, a time of 'emergency' occurred whenever the chief decreed it to be so.

Some clans could muster perhaps a hundred or so broadswords, others several thousand. In all, the total fighting strength of all the Highland clans by the middle of the 18th century amounted to at least 32,000 men (including loyal clansmen). It was well for George II that the entire military might of the mountains did not unite, for if a mere 6,000 marched into the north of England in 1745, producing turmoil in London, one can only presume that an army five times its strength would easily have prevailed. But tradition, ancient feuds, differences in religion and varied political allegiances rendered impossible any sense of common purpose, not least when all these factors are seen in the context of clans often living remotely from one another – as islands unto themselves, quite literally in some cases.

But whatever the cause for which the clan was called out, the chief led it in battle, by right but also by his followers' expectation, for he was the patriarch. The clan gained inspiration from him and the warlike traditions and valorous conduct of their forebears. It relished combat and its concomitant fulfilment of tradition and expression of manhood. In battle it did not merely fight as a unit; father and son, brother and brother fought side-by-side, drawing inspiration from the bravery and hardiness of the others. Everyone occupied his place in the line and held a rank according to his family's status within the clan. The chief served as the colonel, his brothers the equivalents of majors and captains, and the head of each family assumed the role of an officer or NCO. Everyone else filled the ranks, their bonnets bearing the symbol of the clan – a sprig of heather, oak, gale or myrtle – with the most prominent men towards the front, those lowest in the food chain finding themselves progressively further back.

In the fury of action, always accompanied by a piper, the Highlander cried out his clan's slogan, which exhorted the men to close with the enemy in a savage, furious onslaught marked by a panoply of weapons unique to the region, as Defoe described during his time there:

Their ancient arms were the Lochaber ax… It is a tremendous weapon, better to be expressed by a figure than words. They likewise used the broad sword and target: with the latter they covered themselves, and with the first reached their enemies at a great distance. These were their ancient weapons: but, since the disarming act, they are scarcely met with. Partly owing to that, and partly to the spirit of industry now arising among them, the Highlanders, in a few years, will scarcely know the use of any weapon… The dirk was a sort of dagger stuck in the belt. The… arm-pit dagger, was worn there ready to be used on coming to close quarters. These, with a pistol stuck in their girdle, completely armed the Highlanders.

If the English viewed Highlanders as irredeemably uncivilized, they were hard-pressed to apply their prejudices to the chiefs themselves, who not only spoke English as well as (Scots) Gaelic – what contemporaries called Erse – but often acquired facility in French from a tutor or through travel on the Continent. He might boast knowledge of the classics, and ensure that his sons received a good education not merely in Scotland – perhaps in Edinburgh or Glasgow – but in the great cities of Europe. He may have known how to dance a Highland reel, but he was also familiar with the more genteel practices in the south, appreciated French wine and dressed with a view to preserving his Highland identity, but without ignoring symbols of wealth and status like lace around his cuffs and collar. Defoe recognized what others among his countrymen failed to appreciate: that not every Highlander was by definition a thief and a rogue: 'We see every day,' he observed

… gentlemen born here … who are named among the clans as if they were Barbarians, appear at Court and in our Camps and Armies, as polite and as finished gentlemen as any from other countries, or even among our own, and if I should say, outdoing our own in many things, especially in arms and gallantry as well as abroad as at home.

He also lived a lifestyle akin in many ways to his southern counterparts, spending time hunting the rich quarry of stags, wolves and wildcats which populated the glens and watered at the lochs.

The Highland economy naturally reflected the hardness of the geography and the harshness of the region's climate. The glens, characterized by relatively little soil covering rocky ground, offered a correspondingly scarce yield. As Defoe observed, 'By the small proportion of arable land in these parts to the rocks and heaths, the most plentiful year scarce produces sufficient to feed the inhabitants; and consequently, in an unfavourable season, they suffer extreme distress'. This rendered cattle-herding one of the few viable pastoral pursuits. The animals, like the people, come from hardy stock: black, shaggy cows, unlikely-looking creatures which bore up

wonderfully against their harsh
environment, as well as sheep and goats.

The dearth of agriculture and a
dependence on animals goes far in
explaining the Highlanders' military
traditions. Living remote lives with nothing
but their herds to keep starvation at bay,
clansmen by necessity learned to handle
arms to protect their livelihoods, fending
off raiders in the absence of any authorized
individual to uphold the law. Over time
some clansmen applied these skills to more
nefarious purposes and took to stealing
from their neighbours. The cycle of robbery
and violence which followed established
and entrenched a culture of honour; to
Lowlanders and the English, this was little
more than brigandage, whereas to the
Highlanders, disputes between clans
grew into clashes on a considerable scale,
sometimes involving individuals armed with
dirk and sword in deadly single combat, or
occasionally clashes between entire clans.
Over time clans set deeds of heroism and
tales of long-standing rivalry to music and
poetry, reinforcing tribal loyalty, unity and
separateness. 'Vocal music,' Defoe observed,
'was very much in vogue among them, and
their songs were chiefly in praise of their
ancient heroes.'

Such were the people on whom the Stuart
cause chiefly relied for its support – but a
people whose mixed loyalties and motives
denied Prince Charles Edward the full
weight of their numbers. Those mixed
loyalties, some to the Stuarts, others to the
Hanoverians, may be traced to many issues.
The Stuarts, having been Scottish kings as
recently as 60 years before (King James II
having been James Edward Stuart's
grandfather), appealed to many Highlanders
on the basis of cultural identity alone, for
to them there was more natural justice in
lending support to a dynasty with Scottish,
rather than German, roots. Clansmen well
understood the notion put forward by
Charles Edward of rights illegitimately
denied him, for the concept of the rights
and privileges associated with a chief's
power over his clan closely mirrored that

A Highlander on horseback, suggesting a degree of
wealth. A clan's financial well-being varied according
to the productivity of the land which it worked. Every
clansman paid not only fealty to his chief, but his rent
in kind, usually in the form of grain or other commodity.
Their sense of honour stood above all else and they
avenged it on the least provocation, carrying unfulfilled
vendettas from one generation to the next.
(Stuart Reid collection)

of a hereditary king. When that king
simultaneously promised a solution to the
one great political problem about which
even the most isolated Highland clansman
would voice his opinion – the perceived
betrayal of his nation via the Act of Union –
the albeit limited appeal of the Stuart call to
arms becomes apparent. Religion also played
its part; Catholic clans tended to side with
the Jacobite cause, together with many
Episcopalians whose clergy had long before
refused automatically to transfer their loyalty
from one dynastic ruler to the next, rejecting
the oath of allegiance to the Hanoverian
line. Thus, no Highlander can be said to
have fought out of a single motive: some
for religion, others for a political persuasion,
but most out of nothing more complex than
tribal loyalty.

Conclusion and consequences

The aftermath of the rebellion was replete with brutality and wanton destruction. Cumberland treated the Scots as a whole as a conquered people, carrying out purges across Inverness-shire and elsewhere for several weeks after Culloden, leaving desolation over a wide area. In a campaign for which the term 'fire and sword' genuinely applies, government forces destroyed large amounts of food and put to the torch religious structures – Catholic and non-juring Episcopal meeting houses and priests' houses – in a spirit of vengeance and recrimination. Determined to rid the Highlands of all vestiges of resistance, present and future, Cumberland ordered Loudoun to drive off thousands of head of cattle, destroy the ploughs of suspected Jacobite supporters and burn the houses of their leaders. Even when clan after clan surrendered to advancing troops, their submission never guaranteed mercy. The list of atrocities extends too far for any detailed treatment here.

Surviving Jacobite officers generally fled abroad into exile, their lands forfeited to the Crown after being plundered and burnt. As Lord George Sackville wrote:

These hills will now have been thoroughly rummaged, and the inhabitants will have learned that they have placed a vain trust in them [for purposes of refuge]. Those who have submitted have been spared, the others have borne the reward of their own wickedness and obstinacy.

Prince Charles in hiding. He moved around the western Highlands and islands regularly during his months in seclusion, including eight days spent in Ewan Macpherson of Cluny's 'Cage' – a cave overlooking Loch Ericht from the southern slopes of Ben Alder. This abode had two floors covered with moss to keep out the rain. One floor served as a bedroom and the other as a kitchen, the whole guarded by sentries who commanded an excellent view of the surrounding countryside. (Mary Evans Picture Library)

Those rebels who refused to submit found their estates subject to punitive expeditions, leading to the systematic devastation of the country still under the control of the western clans. Even where clansmen submitted and handed weapons in, the suspicions of the authorities often lingered, for many surrendered arms appeared obsolete or rusted, indicating that in fact their serviceable counterparts remained hidden. Cumberland's merciless campaign extended even to the innocent on a number of occasions, when troops harassed those clans that had taken no part in the rebellion and even some known to be loyal to the government. Thousands of cattle were driven to market to be auctioned off while many fugitives, some harbouring Jacobite sympathies and others not, took to the hills where many died of exposure and starvation. Summary justice and atrocities plagued the Highlands for months, with men arbitrarily shot and their wives and daughters raped.

In the aftermath of the rebellion, many tribunals were established throughout the country to try prisoners, some taken in arms and others accused of aiding the rebel forces. After summary trials, convicts went to the gallows, usually a few dozen a day in cities like London, York, Edinburgh, Carlisle and many other places in England and Scotland. The great majority of prisoners were, however, transported to the plantations of the New World. Some died of hunger and disease while awaiting deportation, in transit or in prison awaiting trial, especially those in prison hulks.

Of the most prominent captured rebels, several peers were beheaded and hundreds of commoners hanged. Nevertheless, most Jacobite prisoners had their lives spared, largely under an arbitrary form of justice by which prisoners drew lots and only every 20th man stood trial. Most so peculiarly chosen were found guilty and condemned to death, but in nearly every instance the sentence was commuted to transportation for life as indentured labour. Those not brought to trial could petition for mercy, so long as they pleaded guilty to high treason, in which case

they potentially found themselves sharing the same fate as those who were actually convicted before a court, summary or otherwise.

Thus, the fates of Jacobite prisoners remained largely uniform in this bizarre form of justice, under which about a thousand men were transported and another 200 exiled and banned from ever returning. About 900 further prisoners received their liberty under an Act of Indemnity of 1747, with nearly 400 more having been exchanged for prisoners of war in French captivity. Thus, of the approximately 3,500 Jacobite prisoners whom the official records identify by name, only the fates of about 650 remain mysterious. In all probability, they died in captivity from starvation and disease.

So much for the rank and file of the movement: the fates of the principal Jacobite leaders also demonstrate how completely the rebellion collapsed. As discussed, in the aftermath of Culloden the Prince went on the run, moving from place to place in the western Highlands and islands, with a bounty of £30,000 for anyone able to turn him over to the authorities. He lived on the generosity of a handful of faithful supporters, such as Flora MacDonald. On 20 September 1746 the Prince finally went into exile, boarding the unfortunately named vessel *L'Heureux*, which conveyed him to France. It was the last time he was ever to see Scotland, and would live another 42 years. He remained away from Rome until his

Execution of rebel prisoners at Carlisle. According to a Privy Council decision of May 1746, all trials were to be held in England, which meant that the large number of prisoners held in Inverness were taken by sea to the Thames while others were marched to Tilbury, York or Carlisle. Peers met their fate on the block, commoners at the gibbet and deserters from the British Army before a firing squad. (Author's collection)

father died in January 1766. In time Charles Edward grew more morose, doleful and guilty over the fate that had befallen his faithful Highlanders. As an old man he dissolved into rages if asked about the rebellion, and the Young Pretender ultimately became a sullen, bitter, withdrawn alcoholic. Nevertheless, history has tended to look kindly upon him, emphasizing his

Scotland after Culloden. The destruction of clan power,
but particularly that of their chiefs, combined with
forcible evictions and clearances from the Highlands,
ended a feudal way of life which stretched back many
centuries. (Mary Evans Picture Library)

youthful energy and adventurous side,
leaving little to popular memory other than
his character as the 'Bonnie Prince'. He died
in Rome in 1788, a century after William of
Orange had landed in England to replace
Charles's grandfather on the throne. With
his death the last embers of hope for the
Jacobite cause also died; for although he left
behind him a brother, Henry, Cardinal of
York, he died in 1807 without an heir. By
this time over six decades had passed since
Culloden without any Jacobite stirrings of
any importance.

Lord George Murray never saw the Prince
again after the campaign. He hid for eight
months in Glenartney before fleeing abroad,
travelling through Holland and Italy before
establishing himself in exile in Germany. He
travelled widely and died in Holland in
1760. Lord John Drummond died of fever in
Holland in 1747, while Lord Ogilvy, after a
time in hiding at Loch Wharral in Glen
Clova, made for Norway and then travelled

to France, where he joined the army and
became a general, in time re-establishing
himself in Scotland and dying in 1803. Lord
Elcho fled to France, his estates and title later
forfeited by an Act of Attainder. He served
for many years in the army of Louis XV and
died in Paris in 1787. Lord Pitsligo, who had
hidden with Elcho in Glenshee, remained in
seclusion in Scotland, as did Macpherson of
Cluny, who remained sequestered on Ben
Alder for nine years before leaving Scotland
forever. Lord Lewis Gordon went into exile
to France, went insane, and died in 1756.

Lochiel, who had assisted the Prince as he
wandered, managed also to reach the safety of
France, joining the Bourbon army like many of
his compatriots, including Clanranald,
Lochgarry and others. He died in 1748.
Archibald Cameron, his brother, was executed
in 1753 and appears to have been the last man
to die in the cause of the '45. The Earl of
Kilmarnock and Lords Balmerino and Lovat
also died on the scaffold. The Earl of Cromarty,
although found guilty, was pardoned by the
intervention of the Princess of Wales. The
Marquess of Tullibardine, imprisoned in the
Tower, did not suffer the indignities of a public
execution, for he died of an illness.

In the months which followed Culloden the government in London enacted legislation to stamp out disaffection in the Highlands as vigorously as possible. By the Act of Attainder, aimed at those who played the most prominent part in the rebellion, 41 people were found guilty of high treason. Amongst other pieces of legislation was the Disarming Act, which banned possession of weapons of any kind, as well as punitive legislation against Episcopalians, as so many had supported the Prince. Only small numbers of Episcopalians were allowed to congregate together; their ministers had to take Oaths of Allegiance and Abjuration; notices fixed to church doors indicated that they had submitted to these requirements; and various penalties were decreed, which denied civil rights or imposed prison terms on those who failed to name George II as the king in their prayers, lest it be construed that James Edward Stuart constituted the legitimate sovereign. Other forms of legislation against the Episcopalian Church were enacted and not repealed until 1792, while legislation against the Catholic Church imposed harsh measures as well, concerning the right of inheritance and property bequest and other matters of family law.

Many of the military roads begun by Wade before the rebellion were extended, rendering the Highlands more easily patrolled by small detachments of troops from the regular army or the militia. In time these roads covered almost 1,200 miles, passing over even the most inaccessible regions of the Highlands. In addition, further barracks were constructed, Fort Augustus was repaired and new fortifications erected, most notably Fort George, which took over 20 years to finish. Thousands of troops were dispatched to garrison the Highlands, and the independent companies were disbanded, though they were revived in 1760 during the Seven Years' War (1756–63) with France, and would later be incorporated into the Highland regiments raised for service in Canada, the West Indies and the Continent as part of the regular army. In fact, herein lay the seeds not of reconciliation, perhaps, but of reintegration, for several such regiments were recruited, at once raising the strength of the regular forces and ensuring an outlet for any remaining clan disaffection while at the same time making good use of the Highlanders' martial abilities. By the end of the century 27 regiments of Highlanders had been created for the regular army, with another 19 battalions of militia serving as a reserve – over 30,000 men in total. The integration of the Highlanders into the regular ranks of the British Army did much to soothe the legacy of animosity that remained after 1746 and bring this formerly remote region more closely into the mainstream of British society.

Culloden represented more than the end of the rebellion; it symbolized the end of the Highlanders' way of life. Their defeat signified the end of their struggle to support a Stuart claimant and the euphemistically named 'pacification of the Highlands' destroyed forever much of what made their region distinctive. It constituted more than merely turning much of the area desolate through farm-burning and the wholesale destruction of livestock and crops. In addition to the disarming of the clans, legislation passed at Westminster also abolished the system of heritable jurisdiction, by which Scottish lairds had administered the law on their own estates. Even the Highland national costume was banned, and this was not lifted until 1782:

No man, or boy, within that part of Great Britain called Scotland other than such as shall be employed as Officers and Soldiers in His Majesty's forces shall, on any Pretence whatsoever, wear, or put on Clothes commonly called Highland Clothes; that is to say the Plaid, Philabeg, or little kilt, Trowse, Shoulder-belts, or any part whatsoever of what peculiarly belongs to the Highland Garb.

So comprehensive were government efforts to stamp out the traditions of the Highlands that when in 1773 Dr Johnson toured the west coast he observed a very different society than that which had existed only a generation earlier:

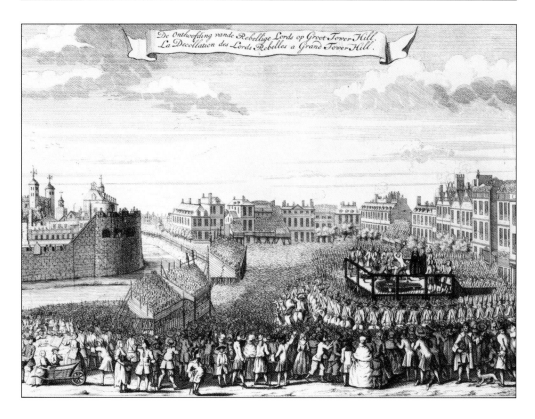

De Onthoofding vande Rebellige Lords op Groot Tower Hill.
La Decollation des Lords Rebelles a Grand Tower Hill.

Execution of rebels at Tower Hill. In the aftermath of the 1745 rebellion, the government sought to reduce the likelihood of another outbreak: in the short term by executing the principal leaders, in the long term by limiting the autocratic powers of the clan chiefs. (Art Archive)

There was perhaps never any change of national manners so quick, so great, and so general as that which has operated in the Highlands by the last conquest and the subsequent laws. We came hither too late to see what we expected – a people of peculiar appearance and a system of antiquated life. The clans retain little now of their original character: their ferocity of temper is softened, their military ardour is extinguished, their dignity of independence is depressed, their contempt of government subdued, and their reverence for their chiefs abated. Of what they had before the late conquest of their country there remains only their language and their poverty.

The balance between progressive and reactionary forces in the Highlands shifted dramatically after 1745, as a result of the government's deliberate policies.

The government abolished hereditary jurisdictions, which although affected all of Scotland, had a particularly profound impact on the Highlands; chiefs lost most of their principal powers over their clansmen, weakening the bonds of the system by striking at the heart of their authority. In addition to this, quite apart from those chiefs held prisoner after Culloden, most of the others had fled abroad and their lands were forfeited to others. They left their clansmen to make the best life they could as tenants of new landlords with no regard for the old ways.

This general exodus did, however, leave room for those landowners loyal to the Hanoverians – or who at least were not overtly hostile and were willing to adapt to new ways. Many tried their hand at new forms of improvement for their agriculture, often with poor results. Whether the post-1745 Acts merely accelerated change or instigated it, by the end of the century Highland chiefs had become akin to their Lowland counterparts, with their former role of patriarch of the clan replaced by one in which care for one's property as a landowner took priority over meeting the needs of the clan.

The clan system could not bear up to such fundamental changes and within a generation it may be said to have died out, as Thomas Pennant noted in his observations of 1769 about the Highlanders:

… their character begins to be more faintly marked; they mix more with the world, and become daily less attached to their chiefs; the clans begin to disperse themselves through different parts of the country, finding that their industry and good conduct afford them better protection … than any their chieftain can afford; and the chieftain tasting the sweets of advanced rents, and the benefits of industry, dismisses from his table the crowd of retainers, the former instruments of his oppression and freakish tyranny.

Nor was this the end of the process of change in the Highlands, which underwent rapid and fundamental social and economic change, not least owing to the Highland Clearances of the end of the 18th century and the early 19th, during which thousands of people were forced off the land in favour of sheep.

***

If the Jacobites failed to achieve their objective, history at least has looked kindly upon them, for most pursued the Prince's cause with little in the way of personal benefit on their minds. Few fought purely out of allegiance to the House of Stuart, but instead, a more general loyalty to their accepted sovereigns – clan and Crown – was the reason most took the field, and they knew that the risks involved in defeat carried with them the ultimate penalty. For this they sought to conquer three kingdoms, with little in their arsenal beyond courage and conviction. Had the government's incompetent strategy for defending England against invasion failed more dramatically, the rebellion might have survived longer, but ultimately the cause was lost.

Oddly, had no fears existed that a Stuart restoration would entail a return to the despotism associated with James II's reign and the arbitrary powers he exercised, the Jacobite cause of his grandson, Charles Edward, might very well have found widespread support across Britain, for the Hanoverians, who came to power 30 years before the '45, could hardly be said to enjoy wide popularity. Only in the latter days of the reign of George III (1760–1820) did the dynasty enjoy general respect.

The great paradox of the 1745 Rebellion was that the men of the losing side, the 'barbarian' Highland clans whose way of life was destroyed in its wake, would in time be seen in a romantic light; noble and ever loyal, for they never betrayed their Prince despite the generous price on his head. The reputation of the Highlands became further enhanced in the latter part of the century when, after faithful service in the ranks of the British Army first against the American revolutionaries (1775–83) and then the French between 1793 and 1815, they not only lost their pariah status but reinvented themselves as some of the most distinguished troops in Georgian service.

Radicalism from France, followed by the still greater threat of Napoleonic expansionism, permanently eradicated any remaining concerns over a renewed Jacobite threat. Indeed, a period of wholesale Celtic revivalism began with George IV's visit to Edinburgh in 1822, when the Hanoverian king wore Highland dress. This process may be said to have been completed by Queen Victoria's regular visits to Balmoral and her genuine fondness for the Highlands. Thus, the social and economic trends which had already begun to transform the rest of Britain in 1746 received a dramatic impetus with the collapse of the Jacobite Rebellion and the reforms undertaken by the government in its aftermath. By the end of the century the Highlanders had undergone a radical transformation; and by the reign of Victoria it had achieved an aura of romanticism which cast the Jacobite cause – now safely at a distance – in a sympathetic light.

Further reading

Note: As the various Jacobite rebellions are related, the following list includes material concerning them all, but with an emphasis on the '45. A wealth of published primary sources also exists.

Barthorp, Michael, *The Jacobite Rebellions* (Osprey, 1982)

Baynes, J. C. M., *The Jacobite Rising of 1715* (Cassell, 1970)

Black, Jeremy, *Culloden and the '45* (Alan Sutton, 1990)

Blaikie, W. B., ed., *The Origins of the '45* (Scottish History Society, 1916)

Bumsted, J. M., *The People's Clearance: Highland Emigration to British North America, 1770–1815* (Edinburgh University Press, 1982)

Coull, Sam, *Nothing But My Sword: The Life of Field Marshal James Francis Edward Keith* (Birlinn, 2000)

Craig, Maggie, *Bare-Arsed Banditti: The Men of the '45* (Mainstream, 2009)

Craig, Maggie, *Damn' Rebel Bitches: The Women of the '45* (Mainstream, 2000)

Cruikshanks, E., ed., *Political Untouchables: The Tories and the '45* (Duckworth, 1979)

Cruikshanks, E., ed., *The Jacobite Challenge* (John Donald, 1988)

Cruikshanks, E. and J. Black, eds., *The Jacobite Challenge* (John Donald, 1988)

Cunningham, A., *The Loyal Clans* (Cambridge University Press, 1932)

Daiches, D., *Charles Edward Stuart: The Life and Times of Bonnie Prince Charlie* (Thames and Hudson, 1973)

Douglas, Hugh, *Jacobite Spy Wars: Moles, Rogues and Treachery* (Sutton, 1999)

Douglas, Hugh and Michael Stead, *The Flight of Bonnie Prince Charlie* (Sutton, 2000)

Duffy, Christopher, *The '45: Bonnie Prince Charlie and the Untold Story of the Jacobite Rising* (Cassell, 2003)

Erickson, Carolly, *Bonnie Prince Charlie: A Biography* (Robson Books, 2001)

Forster, Margaret, *The Rash Adventurer: The Rise and Fall of Charles Edward Stuart* (Secker & Warburg, 1973)

Gibson, John S., *The Ships of the '45: The Rescue of the Young Pretender* (Edinburgh University Press, 1967)

Gibson, J. S., *Lochiel of the '45: the Jacobite Chief and the Prince* (Edinburgh University Press, 1994)

Graham, Henry, *The Social Life of Scotland in the 18th Century* (A & C Black, 1900)

Hill, J. M., *Celtic Warfare, 1595–1763* (John Donald, 1986)

Hook, M. and W. Ross, *The Forty-Five: The Last Jacobite Rebellion* (Edinburgh, 1995)

Hopkins, Paul, *Glencoe and the End of the Highland War* (John Donald, 1986)

Houlding, J. A., *Fit for Service: The Training of the British Army, 1715–1795* (Clarendon Press, 1981)

Hutchinson, R. E., *The Jacobite Rising of 1715* (Scottish National Portrait Gallery, 1965)

Insh, G. P., *The Scottish Jacobite Movement* (P. Moray, 1952)

Kemp, Hilary, *The Jacobite Rebellion* (Altmark, 1975)

Lenman, Bruce, *The Jacobite Risings in Britain, 1689–1746* (Methuen, 1980)

Lenman, Bruce, *The Jacobite Clans of the Great Glen, 1650–1784* (Methuen, 1984)

Lenman, Bruce and John Gibson, *The Jacobite Threat – England, Scotland, Ireland, France: A Source Book* (Scottish Academic Press, 1991)

Lord, Evelyn, *The Stuart Secret Army: English Jacobites, 1689–1752* (Longman, 2004)

Lynch, M., ed., *Jacobitism and the '45* (Historical Society, 1980)

MacInnes, A. I., *Clanship, Commerce and the House of Stuart, 1603–1788* (Tuckwell, 1996)

MacLeod, Ruairidh, *Flora MacDonald: The Jacobite Heroine in Scotland and North America* (Shepheard-Walwyn, 1995)

Margulies, Martin, *The Battle of Prestonpans* (NPI Media Group, 2007)

McClaren, Moray, *Bonnie Prince Charlie* (Rupert Hart-Davis, 1972)

McLynn, Frank, *France and the Jacobite Rising of 1745* (Edinburgh, 1981)

McLynn, Frank, *The Jacobite Army in England 1745* (John Donald, 1983)

McLynn, Frank, *The Jacobites* (Routledge & Kegan Paul, 1985)

McLynn, Frank, *Charles Edward Stuart: A Tragedy in Many Acts* (Routledge, 1988)

Mitchison, R., *Lordship to Patronage: Scotland, 1603–1745* (Edward Arnold, 1983)

Monod, Paul, Murray Pittock and Daniel Szechi, eds., *Loyalty and Identity: Jacobites at Home and Abroad* (Macmillan, 2010)

Oates, Jonathan, *The Jacobite Campaigns: The British State at War* (Pickering & Chatto, 2011)

Oates, Jonathan, *York and the Jacobite Rebellion of 1745* (Borthwick Institute of Historical Research, 2005)

Petrie, C., *The Jacobite Movement* (Eyre and Spottiswood, 1958)

Philipson, N. T. and R. Mitchison, ed., *Scotland in the Age of Improvement* (Edinburgh University Press, 1970)

Pittock, Murray, *Jacobitism* (Macmillan, 1998)

Pittock, Murray, *The Myth of the Jacobite Clans: The Jacobite Army in 1745* (Edinburgh University Press, 2009)

Plank, Geoffrey, *Rebellion and Savagery: The Jacobite Rising of 1745 and the British Empire* (University of Pennsylvania Press, 2006)

Pollard, Tony, *Culloden: The History and Archaeology of the Last Clan Battle* (Pen & Sword, 2009)

Prebble, John, *Culloden* (Penguin, 1967)

Prebble, John, *Glencoe: The Story of the Massacre* (Secker & Warburg, 1966)

Prebble, John, *Mutiny: Highland Regiments in Revolt, 1743–1804* (Secker & Warburg, 1975)

Reid, Stuart, *Culloden Moor 1746: The Death of the Jacobite Cause* (Osprey, 2002)

Reid, Stuart, *Highland Clansman, 1689–1746* (Osprey, 2003)

Reid, Stuart, *Hungry Like Wolves: Culloden Moor, 16 April 1746* (Windrow & Greene, 1994)

Reid, Stuart, *The Scottish Jacobite Army, 1745–46* (Osprey, 2006)

Roberts, John L., *The Jacobite Wars: Scotland and the Military Campaigns of 1715 and 1745* (Polygon, 2002)

Ross, David, *On the Trail of Bonnie Prince Charlie* (Luath Press, 2000)

Salmond, J. B., *Wade in Scotland* (The Moray Press, 1934)

Scott, Andrew, *Bonnie Dundee: John Grahame of Claverhouse* (J. Donald, 2000)

Selby, John, *Over the Sea to Skye* (Hamish Hamilton, 1973)

Simpson, P., *The Independent Highland Companies, 1603–1760* (Constable, 1996)

Sinclair-Stevenson, C., *Inglorious Rebellion: The Jacobite Risings of 1708, 1715 and 1719* (Hamish Hamilton, 1971)

Speck, W. A., *The Butcher: The Duke of Cumberland and the Suppression of the '45* (Blackwell, 1981)

Szechi, Daniel, *1715: The Great Jacobite Rebellion* (Yale University Press, 2006)

Szechi, Daniel, *The Jacobites: Britain and Europe, 1688–1788* (Manchester University Press, 1994)

Tabraham, C. and D. Grove, *Fortress Scotland and the Jacobites* (Batsford, 1995)

Tayler A. and H. Tayler, *1715: The Story of the Rising* (Nelson, 1936)

Tayler A. and H. Tayler, *1745 and After* (Nelson, 1938)

Tomasson, K., *The Jacobite General* (Blackwood, 1958)

Tomasson, K. and F. Buist, *Battles of the '45* (Batsford, 1978)

Whitworth, Rex, *William Augustus, Duke of Cumberland: A Life* (Leo Cooper, 1992)

Whyte, Ian and Kathleen Whyte, *On the Trail of the Jacobites* (Routledge, 1990)

Woosnam-Savage, Robert, ed., *1745: Prince Charles Edward Stuart and the Jacobites* (Stationery Office Books, 1995)

Youngson, A. J., *The Prince and the Pretender: A Study in the Writing of History* (Croom Helm, 1985)

Zimmermann, Doron, *The Jacobite Movement in Scotland and in Exile, 1746–1759* (Macmillan, 2003)

Index

References to illustrations are shown in **bold**.

Aberchalder 10
Aberdeen 10, 11, 14, 42, 47, 55, 61, 62, 67
Alien Act (1705) 18
American Revolution (1775–83) 78, 91
Angus 47, 61
Annan 54
Anne, Queen 16, 18, 20
Ardshiel, chief of 73
Argyll, Earls of 14
Argyll, John Campbell, 2nd Duke of
  16, **20**, 20
Argyll Militia 27, 62, 73
  see also Duke of Argyll's Regiment
Arisaig, Loch nan Uamh 10, 11, 36, **77**
Armadale 75
Atholl, James Murray, 2nd Duke of 63, 65
Attainder, Act of (1746) 89
Atholl Brigade 63
Austrian Succession, War of (1740–48)
  31, 32, 34

Badenoch 67
Balmerino, Lord 44, 88
Banff 47, 67
Bannockburn 55, 56, 60
Beattie, Dr 79
Belle Isle, France 10, **32**
Ben Alder 88
  MacPherson of Cluny's 'Cage' (cave) **85**
Benbecula 76
Berwick-upon-Tweed 17, 46
Blair Atholl 42, 44
Blair Castle 10, 11, 62
Bland, Major-General Humphrey 68, 71
Boulogne 32
Boyne, battle of the (1690) **12**, 13
Braemar **19**, 20
Brampton 48
Breadalbane, John Campbell, 1st Earl of 15
Bridgewater 78
British Army 24–27, 36, 38
  4th Foot (Barrell's regiment) 58, 69
  6th Foot 69
  13th (Gardiner's) Dragoons **42**, 45, 46
  14th Dragoons 45, 46
  37th Foot (Monro's regiment) 69, 70
    corporal 69–70
  44th Foot 45, 46
  46th Foot 45
  47th Foot 45
  artillery 25, 45, 46, 54, 68, 69
  atrocities and wave of destruction after
    Culloden **74**, 85–86
  battalions 24
  and battle of Culloden **67**, 67–69, **70**,
    70, 71–72, 73
  and battle of Falkirk 57, 58, 59
    after battle 59–60, 61, 62
  at battle of Prestonpans 44–45, 46, **49**
  cavalry 25, 54, 68
  cavalry weapons 25
  Cope's troops 40–44, **41**
  deserters 28
  Duke of Argyll's militia 27, 62, 73
  force reaches Newcastle 47
  Guards **25**
  Hessian mercenaries 62
  Highlanders, loyal 26–27, 40, 42, 62, 68
  Highlanders integrated into regular
    ranks 89, 91
  in Highlands after rebellion 89
  independent companies 89
  infantry weapons 24
  and Jacobites' retreat to Scotland 53, 54
  Lord Loudoun's regiment 40, 73
  officers **24**, 26
    promotion of 59

platoon-firing 24
rallies to oppose Jacobites' move south
  47, 49–50
regiments 24
search for Bonnie Prince Charlie after
  Culloden 75, 77
soldiers 25–26
strength when near Stafford 51
training 26
Westmoreland and Cumberland militia
  48
British government 39, 40, 47
  see also House of Commons;
    Parliament, English
Bruges 35
Burt, Edward 80–81, 82

Calais 32
Cameron, Archibald 88
Cameron clan 26–27, 38, 40
Cameron of Lochiel, Donald 36, 38, 67,
  73, 88
Campbell, Sir James 56
Campbell, John, 2nd Duke of Argyll see
  Argyll, John Campbell, 2nd Duke of
Campbell, John, Earl of Loudoun see
  Loudoun, John Campbell, Earl of
Campbell, John, 1st Earl of Breadalbane 15
Campbell clan 14, 15–16, 26–27, 73
Campbell of Glenorchy, John 15
Campbell of Mamore, John 27
Carlisle 11, 17, 48, 49, 50, 51, 54, 55, 64
  siege of (1745) 10, 48, 55
Carlisle Castle 11, 48–49, 54, **87**
Carpenter, General **23**
Catholic Church 89
  meeting/priests' houses 85
Catholics 12, 13, 64, 84
  Irish 13–14
Charles Edward Stuart, Prince (Bonnie
  Prince Charlie – 'Young Pretender') **34**
  acquaints himself with everything
    Scottish 38
  aim to unite whole of Britain behind
    Stuart claim on throne 42, 47
  and battle of Culloden 67–68
    after battle **35**, 73, 74, **85**, 87
  after battle of Falkirk 60
    withdrawal north 61
  birth of 23
  death of 88
  in Edinburgh 43
  and fall of Carlisle 55
  and Flora MacDonald **75**, 75–78, **77**
  in France 34, 35
  gains support from clans **9**, 38
  in hiding **85**, 87
  lack of support from English Jacobites
    50–51, 64, **72**
  lands in Scotland 10, **32**, **33**, 35, 36
  leaves Edinburgh 48
  leaves Scotland 11, **77**, 78, 87
  life after rebellion 87–88
  nominated by father to lead revolt and
    travels to Paris 32–33, 84
  proceeds south 41, 42, 43, 44, 47, 48,
    49, 50
  reads out manifesto **36**
  relations with Lord George Murray
    63, **64**, 64–65
  and retreat to Scotland 11, 53, 54
  Scots support **9**, 36, 38
  voyage to Scotland 10, **32**, 35
Cheek's Creek, North Carolina 78
chronology 10–11
Churchill, John 13
civilian, portrait of 75–78
clan allegiances 16
clan justice structure 81–82, 89, 90

clan loyalties 84
  to the Government **9**, 26
  for Jacobite cause 28, 40, 43–44, 47, 84
clan rivalry 26–27
clan social structure 81
clan support for rebellion 36, 38
clan system dies out 91
Clanranald, MacDonald of 81, 82, 88
Clanranald clan 75
clans, disarming of 89
clans, fighting strength 82
clans in battle 82–83
Clifton 64
  engagement at (1745) 11, 54
Cockenzie 44
Coldstream 46
Congleton 51
Cope, General Sir John 10, 39, 63
  and battle of Prestonpans 44, 45–46, **49**
  Jacobites outmanoeuvre 40–44, **41**
  military chest 46
Corrieyairack Pass 40
Crail 18
Crieff 40, 61, 65
Cromarty, Earl of 88
Cromdale, battle of (1690) 15
Cromwell, Oliver 24
Culloden, battle of (1746) 11, 25, 27, 65,
  67, 67–74, **68**, **69**, **70**, **71**, **72**
  aftermath 73–74, **74**, 85–86, 87
  artillery at 25
  myths dispelled 73
  as symbol of end of Highlanders' way
    of life 89
Culloden Moor 65, 67
  Culchunaig, wall of 71
  Culwhiniac Parks 67, 68
  Leanach 68
Culloden Parks 67
Cumberland (county) 47–48
Cumberland, William, Duke of **7**, **60**
  appointed c-in-c of home forces 47
  assumes command of home forces 51
  atrocities and wave of destruction after
    Culloden 85, 86
  background 59
  and battle of Culloden 25, 67, 69, 71, 72
  at battle of Fontenoy 34
  and Jacobites' retreat to Scotland 11, 53
  and Jacobites' withdrawal north after
    battle of Falkirk 62
  and Murray's diversion 51
  proceeds north to assume command in
    Scotland 11, 59
  promoted to captain-general of British
    land forces in Britain and overseas 59
  reaches Edinburgh 61
  recalled from Flanders 10, 47
  returns to London 11, 54
  suppresses remaining pockets of
    resistance **7**, 11
  victimisation of Highland clans after '45
    rising **60**
Cumbernauld 55

Dalnacardoch 40
Dalrymple of Stair, Sir John 15, 16
Dalwhinnie 40
Declaration of Rights (1689) 13
Defoe, Daniel 79, **80**, 80–81, 83, 84
Derby 11, 51, 64, 65, 66, **72**
  newspaper **53**
Dettingen, battle of (1743) 32, 59, 68
Disarming Act (1746) 89
Dissenters 12
Dornoch, skirmish at (1746) 11
Doune, Castle of **58**
Drummond, James, Duke of Perth
  see Perth, James Drummond, Duke of

Drummond, Lord John 10, 11, 27, 51, 54, 55, 73–74, 88
Du Teillay 32, 35, 36
Duddingston 43, 44
Duke of Argyll's Regiment **15**, 15, 27
    see also Argyll Militia
Dunbar 10, 43
Dundee, John Graham of Claverhouse, Viscount **14**, 15
Dunkirk 18, 19, 32, 34
Durand, Colonel 48

East India Company 18
Ecclefechan 54
Edinburgh 11, 18, 39, 41, 42–43, 46–47, 55, 61, 78
    City Guard 43
    George IV's visit 91
    Jacobite army leaves 48
    Nether Bow port 43
    occupied by Jacobite army 10, 43–44
Edinburgh Castle 20, 42, 43, 44, 46, 48
Elcho, Lord 44, 88
Enlightenment, Age of 79
Episcopalian Church 14, 89
    meeting/priests' houses 85
    ministers 14
Episcopalianism 14–15
Episcopalians 84, 89
Eriskay 32, 33, 35, 36
Erskine, John, 6th Earl of Mar **18**, **20**, 20, **22**
Esk, river 54

Falkirk 11, 55, 58
Falkirk, battle of (1746) 11, 27, 56–59, **57**, **65**, 65–66
Falkirk, Hill of 57–58
Flanders 34, 38, 47, 59
Flodigarry 78
Fontenoy, battle of (1745) 30, 34–35, 56, 59, 68
Forbes of Culloden, Duncan 27, 38–39, 40, 41, 47, 55, 79, 81
Fort Augustus 10, 11, 38, 40, 55, 62, 89
Fort George 38, 61, 89
Fort William 10, 11, 38, 67
Forth, river 42
Fox, HMS 45
Fraser, Simon, Lord Lovat 67, 88
Fraser clan 55
French abortive expedition to Britain (1743) 33–34
French Army 35
    Irish Brigade 13
French expedition (1708) 18–19
French navy 10, 18–19, **32**, 32–33
French support for Jacobites 47, 51, **72**
French support for Stuarts 31
French troops 10, 11, 28, 47, 58, 71
Frew, Fords of 43
Furnace, HMS 78

Gardiner, Colonel James **42**, 44, 46
George I, King 17, 20, 31
George II, King **31**, 35, 38, 59, 82
George IV, King 91
Ghent 35
Glasgow 11, 18, 54
Glasgow Militia 27
Glenartney 88
Glencoe Massacre (1692) **15**, 15–16
Glenfinnan 10, 38, 40
Glenshiel, battle of (1719) **20**, 23, 63
Glorious Revolution (1688–89) 12, 47
Gordon, Lord Lewis 55, 88
Gordon clan 14
Gordon of Glenbucket, John 47
Gorthlick 73
Graham of Claverhouse, John, Viscount Dundee **14**, 15
Grants of Glenmoriston 40
Gravelines 33
Guest, General 42–43

Haddington 43
Hanoverians 16, 17, 38, 91
Hawley, Lieutenant-General Henry 11, 54–55, **55**, 56, 59, 65
    and battle of Culloden 68, 69, 71
    and battle of Falkirk 57, 58, **65**
Hay, John, 4th Marquess of Tweeddale 32
Hazard, HMS 10
Hessian mercenaries 62
Highland Clearances 91
Highland life in mid-18th century 79–84
    chief leads clan in battle 82–83
    chiefs, authority of 82, 90
    chiefs, sophistication of 83
    clan loyalties *see* clan loyalties
    clan social structure 81
    clans, fighting strength 82
    clans in battle 82–83
    clansman and chief, relationship between 82
    descriptions of Highlanders 80–81
    descriptions of Highlands 79–80, **80**, **81**
    farming 83–84
    law, application of 81–82
    military traditions 84
    music and poetry 84
    religion 84
    tenants 82
    tribal system 79
Highland national costume banned 89
Highlanders **29**, 84
    descriptions of 80–81
        after rebellion 91
    dress 28, 29, 29, **53**, **65**, **68**, 80–81, **84**, 89
    and firearms **27**
    loyalist 26–27, 40, 42, 62, 68
    retreat from Perth 62
    tactics 29–30
    way of life, end of 89–90, 91
Highlands, 'pacification' by British troops 73–74, 87, 89–90
Highlands, wave of destruction after battle of Culloden **7**, **11**, 73–74, **74**, 85–86, 87, **88**
Hogarth, William **25**
Home, Lord 46
House of Commons 12, 31–32, 59
    see also British government; Parliament, English
Huske, General 56, 70

Indemnity, Act of (1747) 86
Inverness 10, 11, 20, 40–41, 42, 55, 61, 62
Inverness-shire 85
Inverurie, engagement at (1745) 11
Ireland 13, 14
Irish Brigade in French Army 13
Irish Catholics 13–14
Irish troops 10, 51

Jacobite army 28–30, **39**
    artillery 30
    Atholl Brigade 63
    and battle of Culloden **67**, 67, 68–71, **70**, 72–73
        after battle **7**, **11**, 74
        atrocities committed against after battle 73–74, **74**, 85–86, 87, **88**
    and battle of Falkirk 56, 57–59
        withdrawal north after 59–62, 64, 65–66
    and battle of Prestonpans **9**, 10, 44, **45**, 45–46, **49**
    British Army deserters 28
    cavalry 30
    Council of War 49, 51, 61, 65
    crosses Forth 42
    deserters 11
    dress style 29, **53**
    Fitzjames' Horse 30
    infantry tactics 29–30
    lack of support in England 50–51, 64, **72**

Lady Mackintosh's Regiment **68**
Lord Kilmarnock's Horse Grenadiers 30
Lord Pitsligo's Horse 30
    march south 10, 41, 42, 43, 44, 46–51, 64
    occupies Edinburgh 10, 43–44
    officers 28, 29, 30
        French Army 54
        senior **28**
    regiments 28–29
    reinforcements arrive from France 51, 54
    retreats to Scotland 11, 51, 53–56
    Royal Scots 27
    soldiers 28
    strength on leaving Edinburgh 48
    weapons **29**, 29
Jacobite Rebellion (1715) 20, **22**, 22–23, **23**, 31, 61, 63
Jacobite Rebellion (1745–46)
    aftermath 73–74, 85–91
        atrocities and wave of destruction in Highlands **7**, **11**, 73–74, **74**, 85–86, 87, **88**
        government legislation 89
        Highland national costume banned 89
        Highlanders integrated into regular army ranks 89
        leaders, fate of **87**, 87–88, **90**, 90
        'pacification' of Highlands 73–74, 87, 89–90
        prisoners, fate of 86, **87**, **90**
        trials and transportations 86, **87**
    and battle of Culloden **67**, 67–74, **70**
    and battle of Falkirk 56–59, **57**
        withdrawal north after 59–62
    and battle of Prestonpans **9**, 10, 44–46, **45**, **49**
    French abortive expedition to Britain (1743) 33–34
    French support 47, 51, **72**
    and Jacobites' march south 46–51
    and Jacobites' retreat to Scotland 51, 53–56
    occupy Edinburgh 10, 43–44
    outbreak 31–35
        French support for Stuarts 31
    outmanoeuvring Cope 38–44, **41**
    raising the standard **36**, 36, 38, 40
    troop movements, major **52**
    voyage to Scotland 10, **32**, 35
Jacobitism, roots of 12–20, 22–23
    and Act of Union 17, 18, 19
    battle of Killiecrankie **14**, 15
    clan allegiances 16
    and Episcopalianism 14–15
    first revolt led by Viscount Dundee (1689) **14**, 15
    Glencoe Massacre **15**, 15–16
    Jacobite community in Europe 13–14
    and James VII 12, 13, 14
    rebellion (1715) 20, **22**, 22–23, **23**, 31, 61, 63
James VII of Scotland (James II of England) **12**, 12, 13, 14, 15, 17, 18, 88, 91
James Edward Stuart, Prince ('Old Pretender') **17**, 38, 65, 87
    before Jacobite Rebellion (1745–46) 12, 16, 17, 18, 19–20, 22, 23, 32
Jedburgh 48
Jenkins' Ear, War of (1739–48) 31
Johnson, Dr Samuel 79–80, **81**, 89–90
Johnstone, Chevalier de 46, 74
Johnstone, James 71

Keith 11, 62
Keith, George, 10th Earl Marischal 33
Kellie, Earl of 44
Kelso 48
Kendal 11, 53
Keppoch, MacDonald of 67, 73
Killiecrankie, battle of (1689) **14**, 15
Kilmarnock, Earl of 88

Kilsyth 55
Kingsburgh House 78

L'Elisabeth 10, **32**, 35
L'Heureux **77**, 87
Lancashire 49, 50
Leith 40, 42
Lichfield 51
Limerick, Treaty of (1691) 13
Linlithgow 11, 43, 56, 58
Lion, HMS 10, **32**, 35
Loch Ericht, MacPherson of Cluny's 'Cage'
    (cave) **85**
Loch nan Uamh, Arisaig 10, 11, 36, **77**
Loch Shiel 10, 38, 40
Loch Skipport 75–76
Loch Snizort 77
Loch Wharral 88
Lochgarry, chief of 88
Lochiel, Donald Cameron of 36, 38, 67,
    73, 88
London, Tower Hill **90**
Loudoun, John Campbell, Earl of 11, 26,
    40, 44, 46, 62, 67, 73, 85
    regiment 40, 73
Louis XIV, King of France 13, 16, 18, 22
Louis XV, King of France 10, 31, 38, 47
Lovat, Simon Fraser, Lord 67, 88

McBean, Major Gillies **68**
MacDonald, Aeneas 35, 36
MacDonald, Allan 78
MacDonald, Flora **75**, 75–78, **77**, 87
    father 75
    life after her release 78
    mother 75
    questioned and confined after Bonnie
        Prince Charlie's escape 78
    stepfather 75
MacDonald, Lady Margaret 77
MacDonald clan 15–16, 38, 54, 67
MacDonald of Castleton, Donald 78
MacDonald of Clanranald 81, 82, 88
MacDonald of Keppoch 67, 73
MacDonald of Kingsburgh, Alexander 7–78
MacDonald of Sleat, Alexander 36, 75, 77
MacDonalds of Clanranald 36, 40, 81, 82
MacDonalds of Glengarry 40
MacDonalds of Keppoch 38, 67, 73
MacEachain, Neil 75, 77–78
MacGregor clan 42, 67
Mackenzie clan 67
Mackinnon or Mackinnon 47
Maclachlan clan 44
Maclain, Alasdair **15**, 15
MacLean clan 26–27
MacLeod clan 38, 55, 77
    chief of 36
MacLeod of Bracadale, Captain Alexander
    77
Macpherson of Cluny, Ewan 42, 62, 73,
    85, 88
Malplaquet, battle of (1709) 19
Manchester 10, 51, 53
Mar, John Erskine, 6th Earl of **18**, **20**,
    20, **22**
Marischal, George Keith, 10th Earl 33
Marlborough, John Churchill, Duke of 13
Mary, Queen 13, 15
Moffat 48
Moidart 36
Monkstadt (formerly Mugstot) House 77
Montrose 10, 29, 47
Moore's Creek Bridge, battle of (1776) 78
Moy Castle 11
Mugstot (now Monkstadt) House 77
Munro of Culcairn, George 42
Murray, Lord George 11, 30, 42, 55, **56**,
    63–66, **64**
    advance into England 10–11
    appointed joint commander 10
    background 63
    and battle of Culloden 65, 68, 71
        after battle 65, 73–74, 88

and battle of Falkirk 57, **65**
    withdrawal north after 61, 62, 65–66
and battle of Prestonpans 44, 46
death of 88
leadership style 66
and logistics 63–64
marches to Congleton as diversion 51
and move south 47–48
moves against Hawley 11, 55
qualities as commander 63, 66
after rebellion 65, 73–74, 88
relations with Bonnie Prince Charlie
    63, **64**, 64–65
and retreat to Scotland 54
and return north 64, 66
Murray, James, 2nd Duke of Atholl 63, 65
Murray, William 63
Murray of Broughton, John 36, 38, 63

Nairn 11, 67
Newcastle-upon-Tyne 10, 17, 47, 49, 53
Norris, Admiral Sir John 33, 34, 59

officers, British Army **24**, 26
officers, Jacobite army 28, 29, 30
    senior **28**
Ogilvy, Lord 47, 88
Ostend 35
O'Sullivan, Colonel John 35, 63
Oudenarde, battle of (1708) 19

Paris 32–33, 34
Parliament, English 13, 17–18
    see also British government;
        House of Commons
Parliament, Scots 17, 18
Patterson, Thomas 48
Peebles 48
Penduin 78
Pennant, Mr 80
Pennant, Thomas 91
Penrith 53–54
Perth 10, 11, 20, 42, 54, 55, 62
    Highlanders retreat from **62**
Perth, James Drummond, Duke of 10, 36,
    38, 42, 48, 51, 60, 62, 63, 64, 73–74
Peterhead 10, 29
Philip V, King of Spain 23
Pitsligo, Lord 47, 88
Plean Muir 57
Portree 78
Presbyterian Church 19
    General Assembly 14
Presbyterianism 14, 18
Preston, England 20, **23**, 49, 50–51, 53, 64
Preston, Scotland 44
Preston House park 44
Prestonpans 44
Prestonpans, battle of (1745) **9**, 10, 29, **42**,
    44–46, **45**, **49**, 59, 63
Prince de Conti **77**
Protestants 12
Prussians 31, 34

Raasay 78
Robertson clan 42
Rome 22, 31, 32, 65, 88
Roquefeuille, Admiral 33–34
Rossinish 76
Royal Ecossois regiment 28
Royal Navy 10, 18–19, **32**, 35, 45, 67, 78
    Channel squadron 33
Ruthven 40, 65, 73, 74
Ruthven Barracks 10, 11
Ryswyck, Treaty of (1697) 16

Sackville, Lord George 85
Saxe, Marshal de 33, 34, 38
Scotland, map of **37**
    Inverness to Aberdeen area of operations
        61
Scotland, hereditary jurisdictions abolished
    89, **90**
Security, Act of (1703) 17, 18

Settlement, Act of (1701) 16–17
Seven Men of Moidart 35
Seven Years' War (1756–63) 89
Sheridan, Sir Thomas 35
Sheriffmuir, battle of (1715) **20**, 20, **22**, 56
Skye 36, 47, 76–78
Sleat 78
soldier, portrait of 63–66
Sophia, Electress of Hanover 17
South Uist 75
    Sheaval Hill 75
Spanish expedition to Britain (1719) **20**, 23
Spanish Succession, War of (1701–14) 17
Spey, river 11
Staffordshire 10
Stair, Earl of 59
Stewarts of Appin 26–27, 40
Stewarts of Ardshiel 38, 73
Stirling 11, 40, **42**, 46, 49, **55**, 55, 56, 65
Stirling Castle 11, **58**
    siege of (1746) 11, **55**, 55–57, **56**, 60–61
Stonehaven 47
Strathallan, Lord 51, 54
Strickland, Francis 35
Stuart, Henry, Cardinal of York 88
Stuart, Prince Charles Edward see Charles
    Edward Stuart, Prince
Stuart, Prince James Edward see James
    Edward Stuart, Prince
Stuart dynasty 31, 84
Sutherland 67
Sutherland, Earl of 20
Sutherland, Earls of 14, 20

Talbot, Richard, Earl of Tyrconnell 13
Taybridge 40
Tournai 35
Tranent 44
Tranent Meadows 44
Treatise on Discipline 68
Trotternish 77
Tullibardine, William, Marquess of 23, 35,
    38, 48, 63, 73–74, 88
Tullibardine Castle 65
Tweeddale, John Hay, 4th Marquess of 32
Tyrconnell, Richard Talbot, Earl of 13

Ulster 13
Union, Act of (1707) 17, 18, 19, 20, 38,
    47, 84
Utrecht, Treaty of (1713) 19–20, 22

Victoria, Queen 91

Wade, Field Marshal George 11, 29, 48, 49,
    50, 51, 65
    assembles troops at Newcastle 10, 47
    and Jacobites' retreat north 53
    military roads 40, **50**, 80, 89
Wakefield 53
Wales, Princess of 88
Walpole, Sir Robert 31–32
Walsh, Antoine 35
Waternish Point 76–77
weapons
    British Army
        artillery **25**, 45, 46, 54, 68, 69
        cavalry 25
        infantry 24
    Highlanders **27**, 83
    Jacobite army 29, **29**
        artillery 30
Whigs 32
Whitefoord, Colonel 46
Whitney, Colonel 46
Wiay 76
Wigan 11, 53
Wightman, General **20**, 23
William of Orange (later William III), King
    12–13, 14, **15**, 15, 16, 88
Wills, General **20**, **23**
Wolfe, James 26, 70

Yorke, Joseph 69